I0411648

Working through the foster

care system:

My journey as a social worker

By Regan Matthews

ISBN: 1511680067
ISBN-13: 978-1511680066

DEDICATION

This book is for all of the social workers out there who would have enjoyed putting their experiences to paper, but became too overwhelmingly busy to do so. And to all of the foster parents out there who are doing the "foster parent" term justice. I salute you!!!

CONTENTS

ACKNOWLEDGEMENTS

This book would never have come to fruition without the many experiences I have had over the past nine years. I also want to acknowledge my family, my mother, my two fathers, my husband, and my awesome co-workers (you know which ones you are!!), for always being supportive of me, whether with my work as a social worker, or encouraging me to follow my dreams of writing. Thank you for putting up with my weirdness and craziness over the years.

1

Introduction

For years, I have often been asked questions based on my experience what to expect from the foster care system from family and friends. My experience as a social worker is limited to the nonprofit adoption and foster care perspective. I know little to nothing about general domestic adoptions (such as a birth mother willingly puts her baby up for adoption prior to birth, usually with a parent or couple selected prior to the birthing experience) or international adoptions. Throughout the years of my experience, there have been many changes through the agency I have worked for as well as through the foster care system in general. The problem with the foster care experience is there is no one typical experience. Every case, and child, is unique. My intention is to explain a view of the adoption and foster care experience from a agency social worker's standpoint. But first, my credits to the following perspective on the foster care system.

I was in the process of earning my masters in counseling when I needed to find a way of earning my intern hours in order to complete my program. One of my classmates approached me to apply at her agency where she was a social worker and in the process of advocating for a clinical piece. My educational program was focused on the Marriage and Family Therapist track, where the ultimate obvious goal was to eventually be licensed as a Marriage and Family Therapist.

Before I continue, I think it should be noted that there appears to be a rift between the social work track and the therapist track. At one point, an organization was trying to justify why an individual with a counseling degree does not hold the proper qualifications to be employed as a social worker as an individual with a social work degree would. This may have been due to a shortage of social worker positions open, and being filled by individuals with other degrees than social work degrees. However, I have become aware that many open social worker positions today specify a master's degree in social work as a requirement. It does little justice for those on a different track who have been great social workers for years. But that is another chapter.

I also must note that up to this point in my working life, I swore I would never be a social worker. I had my own perceived perceptions of the social work arena. Running down paperwork at every turn, making frivolous calls like a client's own personal planner and customer services representative. Although my perceptions would later prove to be somewhat valid, I was also way off in other perspectives.

I agreed to apply for an open position at the agency, figuring it would be a win-win situation if I miraculously got the job. Unlike many internship opportunities at that time, I would be able to get paid for my internship and have a fulltime job all in one. Other students in the same program, past and present, would be stuck working for their internship hours for free in addition to their already fulltime employment. Many organizations love the intern who they can squeeze "free" work out of at any opportunity. The pay grade was much higher, more than double, my then income, even at the below base level pay. As a beginner with no direct social work experience as well as a master's degree in progress, I could get paid at the lowest entry level pay grade for a Monday through Friday, 8-5 work week (which was still fantastic for the lowly worker who was making $8 an hour for random shifts).

I began as a foster care social worker, who worked mainly with children in long term foster care, reunification, and emancipation. I was a foster care social worker for two years before I was approached by an adoption social worker with the agency to apply for a newly opened adoption position. Because of my above par writing skills, I got the position. I would proceed to work directly in adoptions for the next five years. I assessed families to determine if they were able and willing to provide a permanent family for foster children and youth, whether related or not. After an extreme change in expectations, and unrealistic ones, I clashed with my supervisor and returned back to foster care where I have been since July 2013. Although I currently am considered a foster care social worker once again, I continue to be sought out for adoption related questions and expertise from my fellow co-workers and foster families. During the first six years of my employment, I was involved in weekly clinical groups with a local therapist contracted by the agency to provide clinical supervision hours for both social workers on the MFT track as well as the social work track.

I have become disillusioned with the "system" as it were and continue to look for ways to re-spark my passions for the work I do. This journey is part of my intentions of sharing my knowledge while seeking out that spark again. It takes a special kind of individual to be involved in the foster care and adoption processes, as you will soon learn. It's hard to just walk away from this kind of work, yet it manages to burn people out in the field quickly. Passion and commitment are a necessity in this field. Now, let's begin a journey.

"There are just under 60,000 children and youth in foster care in

California—by far the highest population of any state."   --SFCASA.org

2

What Permanency Looks Like

Permanency, and it's meaning, has morphed over the years. 20 to 30 years ago, a child or youth remaining "in the system" as a foster child was a typical permanency plan that left no one the wiser. However, it has since been researched that working with a birth family to maintain a child or children's placement with the family is more beneficial in the long run, regardless of how chaotic or stressful it may be. Unfortunately, however, once a danger is presented, child protective workers and the courts have to respond immediately whether or not research suggests remaining with birth family is in the child's best interest. Further research has found that leaving a child or children in the "system" for any great length of time becomes damaging in the long run. While remaining with the immediate birth family, family maintenance services are provided by the county. If removal

from the birth family's care is eminent, the following permanency plans are

as followed, in order: family reunification, adoption/legal guardianship,

and/or emancipation.

Family Maintenance

Family maintenance occurs when a family has been identified as on the

threshold of becoming a part of the "system." Child Protective Services

(CPS) steps in and initially provides support, resources, and other services

to maintain a child's, or children's, placement in the home, unless eminent

danger determines immediate removal. The family is given a timeline,

which depends on the workers involved as well as the court system, to

begin and complete a specific plan in order to "graduate" out of CPS'

involvement. If the family makes little headway in their case plan, a child or

children can be removed. People often ask why other family members

cannot take children of such a situation. The answer is they can. However,

if police and child protective services become involved before a family

member can step up, then the process becomes more complicated. For an

example, if a mother leaves her children with the grandmother for extended

periods of time, and the grandmother accepts this responsibility, the police

and child protective services do not become involved, and the children can

continue to remain with the grandmother uninterrupted with little to no involvement with CPS. However, if children are removed from the mother from this example by the police and/or CPS, and if the grandmother still wishes to be involved after the children have been removed from care, she now must do so with the involvement of CPS.

Family Reunification

If a child or children are removed from their immediate birth family by the police or CPS, the typical initial case plan becomes family reunification. The child or children are placed with a foster family or extended relatives, as a foster child. Family can take placement of the children, but must go through the county of dependency's process to pass a background assessment, sometimes similar to that of foster parents, but less intensive. I say county of dependency because if a child lives in one county, but is visiting another county at the time of removal while in the birth parent's care, the child becomes a dependent of the court where the child was physically removed. Some counties can work a plan to have the child brought under the care of the county they are originally part of, where they normally reside, but this occurs infrequently. This is why some birth families that are on their local county's radar may leave the county in an attempt to avoid CPS involvement, only to have the new county step in when an issue arises. I have seen this scenario occur a handful of times.

Family reunification usually includes any of the following expectations of the birth parent or caregiver: regular attendance at scheduled birth family visits, finding and maintaining a residence and employment, random drug testing, participating in therapy, support groups, parenting classes, or other identified resources, attending court hearings, eliminating relationships with significant others (such as in domestic violence cases), entering drug treatment, or any other specified goal relevant directly to the case. Case plans are generally reviewed at court every six months. A change has occurred in this arena where some counties will not allow reunification services to extend longer than 18 months, especially in those cases where the child is under three years old. Another case is if the birth parent has already lost several other children to the system. However, it depends on certain factors, such as progress, if any, by the birth parents, age of the child or children, and the judge on the case. This timeline can be complicated if a family had been involved in the "system", had their case "closed", but end up re-entering the "system," thus starting the 18 month period over again. If a child or children reunify with the birth family, the case is not officially "closed," and CPS becomes involved again and must remove the child or children, the 18 month timeframe usually continues without interruption. However, as mentioned before, several factors can determine this and is in no way a set rule of thumb.

Family reunification can be complicated for foster parents, even relative caregivers. Depending on the timeline in the process, there are generally visits scheduled. Visits can range from one hour a day one day a week, to overnight visits on the weekends. Visits can be scheduled a few days a week, a few hours a day, early in the family reunification process as well as towards the end of the process. In some cases, multiple visits are scheduled to accommodate different individuals involved in the child or children's life. In a domestic violence case, for example, visits with the birth mother and birth father are separated because technically the couple is not supposed to be interacting per their case plan. Visits can become time consuming on any person's time and patience. While in family reunification, the foster family is expected to be accommodating, flexible, and adaptable, even in the most overrated circumstances. It is a complaint agency social workers hear on a consistent basis.

One thing I tell foster families who have a child or children in family reunification is that they need to expect the county and courts to go above and beyond to provide the birth family ample opportunities for success, even at the expense of others. When a birth family fails their case plan, with the ultimate plan of relinquishing a parent's parental rights, a county and court system has to be able to demonstrate that all opportunities were offered and presented to the birth family, and the failure of the plan lies solely on the birth family. Family reunification is the most ideal permanency plan of them all. Children are reunified with their birth family, who hopefully took advantage of the resources given to them in a desperate time in order to be able to later provide for their family where as they were once unable to, regardless of the reason why. Truthfully, some people just have difficult times in their lives where they could use extra support and extra help, but do not know how to find it or who to ask it from. Not all birth families who have children removed from their care are horrid, uncaring, selfish, evil individuals as are often portrayed or assumed.

Adoption

The second most ideal permanency plan is adoption. The purpose of adoption is to build a permanent "forever" home for a child rather than string him or her along in years of back and forth trauma in long term foster care. Staying in long term foster care has been researched to be damaging in the long run. Adoption makes the child a permanent part of a "forever" family with lifelong connections that will not disappear just because a birth parent wants, or needs, to walk away. Adoption can be a wonderful experience, for the adoptive parents as well as the adopted child. But one thing that I must iterate is, you cannot walk through life and say that these children, foster children, only need love. True, they do need love, but it takes more than just love to make a caring, productive individual. Adoption can also be another stressful event for a child who has already experienced other stressful life events. Adoption is much more complex than people realize. Parents do not come swooping in, cradling their new adopted child in their arms, saving him or her from the bad monsters of the past, and then live happily ever after. Adoption is a new journey all in itself.

At some point during the 18 month trial period of reunification, or shortly thereafter, the county and courts are looking for a permanency plan in the event that the family reunification should fail. If an adoptive home has already been identified, the child or children must have been living with the potential adoptive family for at least six months to determine stability and wellness of fit (the family fits with the child and the child fits with the family). As long as a child has been in a stable home for at least six months, the adoption plan can proceed. What I tell families I have worked with in the past, in a best case scenario situation, from placement to adoption finalization, an adoption plan averages two years. However, the timeframe changes due to several different factors along the way.

The court must change the case plan in court at the review hearing from reunification to adoption. An adoption county worker is assigned to the case, which can also take time, depending on the caseloads of the county's workers at any given time. A homestudy, or assessment of the adoptive family, is completed if one has not already been completed. Some counties will not proceed with an adoption plan until the homestudy report has been written already or an old one updated. A court hearing, called the .26 hearing, is scheduled to terminate the parental rights of the birth parents. Once the hearing for the termination of rights occurs, the birth parent or parents have 60 days to appeal the ruling. If the birth parent appeals the ruling, further court reviews will play out until the appeal is deemed appropriate with the birth parent maintaining involvement or deemed inappropriate at which time the court can terminate rights and proceed with adoption. I am often asked how likely it is that birth parents appeal their rights, and how often these appeals are upheld. Honestly, I have only heard of a handful of cases, none mine, where a birth parent or birth parents appealed the ruling. On those exceptionally rare occasions have I ever heard, usually in the news from another state, that an appeal has been up-held. This part of the process is what tends to scare potential adoptive parents the most. I cannot say it never happens because it very well can. However, in five years of direct adoption work, I personally never had a case that an appeal was upheld or delayed an adoption for very long.

Once rights have been terminated, the county prepares for the next phase in the adoption process. This is called the adoptive placement. Most foster children from the child welfare system are eligible for state adoption funding after the adoption occurs. This is a little known fact that tends to be looked over, but I find it a relevant piece of information that those who want to adopt should know. The county has a process where they determine if a child is eligible for the adoption assistance program. If a child is eligible, the child is eligible for the following: Medi-Cal coverage until the age of 18 years old (if a parent puts the child on their own medical coverage, Medi-Cal will remain as a secondary insurance); adoption assistance program (AAP) funding (adoptive parent is paid a monthly payment/stipend determined based on the child's age at the time of adoption until the child turns 18 years old, unless there is a documented special need that allows the funding to continue to the age of 21); adoptive parent receives a tax credit the year of the adoption (for example, a child is adopted in November 2014, when filing taxes in 2015, the parent can use the tax credit, usually ranging from $9,000 to $12,000, and can be carried over across five years); foster parents can be reimbursed for up to $400 on adoption expenses such as for co-pays on physical exams, TB tests, fingerprinting, etc.; and ability to contact the post adoption unit of the county of dependency for resources after adoption such as for adoption camps, support groups, therapy, short term placement at a group home, or psychotropic medication concerns.

If a youth is 13 or older at the time of adoption, when he or she completes their FAFSA to apply for financial aid for college, the youth can claim themselves as an independent. This means they do not claim any parent figure for income purposes. By being able to do this, the youth can receive multiple financial resource opportunities, and can possibly have a free ride through a college education.

A new benefit in order to encourage the adoption of older youth was developed around the time of AB 12. Although AB 12 will be discussed in detail later, the benefits of a youth adopted after the age of 16 years old will be discussed here. There are similarities with the adoption of youth 16 and older and with the youth that qualify for AB 12 benefits. If a youth is adopted at or after the age of 16 years old, he or she still qualifies for Medi-Cal benefits until the age of 21 years old. The adoptive parents also will continue to receive AAP funding until the youth is 21 years old if the following occurs: the youth must continue residing in the home, and the youth must be working and/or the youth must be attending school. When the youth leaves the home, is no longer working and/or is not attending a school, the AAP funding will cease. Like the youth 13 and older, the 16 and older adopted youth qualify for the college benefits while applying as an independent.

Once an adoption has occurred, the family is able to contact the county of dependency at anytime until the child or youth reaches 18 years of age should the need for more support or resources becomes an issue. The county of dependency is available for resources such as therapy options, camps or activities that are provided for adoption children from their county, and other resources for behavioral or developmental need concerns. What I tell families who are at the adoptive placement stage is that should issues arise later that are not relevant at the time of adoption such as the need for therapy or medications, take the child or youth and get the process started with the need or service, and then contact the county of dependency to determine if there are other resources and benefits the county can assist with, such as a raising the AAP funding per month to offset the adoptive parent's cost for services. However, documentation for the need is required.

Legal Guardianship

I often refer to legal guardianship as the counties' best kept secret. In 2013, a big push began with legal guardianship as the alternative to adoption. Most counties will not even suggest legal guardianship as an alternative until the last resort. The counties' goal is to ultimately get children out of the "system" any way they can. This has led to changes that have included mentors becoming caregivers, such as school teachers or coaches, seeking "non- relative extended family member" (referred to as NREFM), seeking relatives out of state whether or not they have met the child or not, and legal guardianship.

There are two types of guardianship, one with dependency and one without. Guardianship with dependency maintains more active involvement from the county. Visits still occur with a county worker, as frequent as every month up to every six months. The court usually can and will still enforce visitations to occur, as frequently as once or twice a month with the birth family. Another little known secret is the funding associated with legal guardianship. This is where the lines turn gray. Those who have taken legal guardianship in the past that I have met did not qualify for funding due to higher income brackets. However, recent changes have included the legal guardianship rates to parallel those of the adoption assistance funding rate. Another gray area here is that many county workers know as much about the legal guardianship specifics as I do, which often feels like next to nothing at times. I have seen a county not provide a guardianship rate at all in one case that I became aware of indirectly. I have also heard situations from fellow agency adoption social workers where the guardianship rate was lower than the rates we had been informed with.

Guardianship has been key where family members do not want to adopt. Many relatives hold high hopes that the birth parent will "get their act together" and get custody of their child or children back. Guardianship is also a permanency plan best suited for older youth who choose not to be adopted, but do not want to remain in the foster care system either. There have been rare, but more frequent cases of foster parents taking legal guardianship of younger children if the birth parents wish to remain involved and the foster parents do not wish to adopt. By taking guardianship, there are fewer professionals involved.

Emancipation and AB 12

Even with the existence of AB 12, emancipation still exists. Emancipation occurs when a foster youth ages out of the foster care system on the 18th birthday. The running joke is that the youth has one foot ready to step out the door at midnight or 12:01 a.m. on the day of the 18th birthday. Unfortunately though, this is no laughing matter. It has been commonly described that foster children and foster youth are waiting to emancipate from the day they are put in to the foster care system. An extension to the age of 19 years old can occur if there is a possibility of graduating high school by that time or shortly after.

Each year over 4,000 foster youth emancipate in California. They lack a supportive network of adults and generally have no plan for work or housing.

Within the first 2 to 4 years after "aging out" of the system, 51% of these young adults are unemployed, 40% are on public assistance, 25% become homeless, and 20% will be incarcerated. (SFCASA.org)

Based on research and studies over the decades, it has been proven that emancipation has not always been a positive experience. Teen pregnancies are higher among females who were a part of the foster care system. From personal experience, there were at least two females within our specific site that became pregnant during care in the foster home. There were also several other reports of former foster youth who ended having children shortly after emancipation, anywhere from months to a year or two after leaving care.

The population of the homeless is made up of a rather high percentage of former foster youth. A high percentage of former foster youth end up committing crimes, and going to jail. During my eight plus years as a social worker, our entire agency experienced anywhere from half a dozen to a dozen deaths of former foster youth, causes ranging from car accidents, drug overdose, unknown medical causes, and suicide. Emancipated youth often run back to their birth families, the same ones that lost custody of them in the first place. Or, as we say in the business, youth "couch surf" until they burn their bridges with the people who have taken them in.

Because of the rising concerns surrounding emancipated youth, Assembly Bill 12 (AB 12), or the California Fostering Connections to Success Act, was passed in October 2010 (California Youth Connection). The first year the Bill took effect was January 1, 2012. With hiccups along the way for those first few years as with most new projects and programs, the Bill has been a blessing in disguise for some youth. Youth could choose to stay in foster care, or in some sense a part of the child welfare system to some degree, and take advantage of the increasing benefits from the Bill. It is a voluntary program. These youth are often referred to as non-minor dependents.

A youth could choose from the following scenarios: live in a foster home, live with a roommate or other people (usually as long as none of these people were the birth family in which the youth was removed from care as the county involved must approve the placement), live in a dwelling on his or her own, in a group home, a specified transitional living program, or in a college dorm room. A common factor across the living scenarios was the common rules to follow. A youth must be attending high school, attending college or a technical program, and/or employed. A youth can remain an AB 12 participant until 21 years of age. Because the youth is still technically a dependent of the child welfare system, regular court hearings continue every six months to check in on progress and participation.

One of the areas that has been cause for concern with non-minor dependents is the free ability to leave foster care at the age of 18 years old, or anytime thereafter, with the ability to return as long as the youth is under the age of 21 to take advantage of the AB 12 benefits as long as they follow the basic rules noted above. The hiccup in this theory is the blank period of the goings-on for the youth prior to re-entry. A youth could go on a crime spree and return to care without the foster parent, or foster care agency, having any right to be privy to this information. Another hiccup is when the youth did not previously know the foster parents in any fashion prior to moving in. The first few cases of experience in AB 12 youth from our agency's standpoint were from youth who were already living with the foster parents that they choose to remain with, or a youth who has been in the agency's care before, so there is a common known history. The youth with the question marks in their past, regardless of how recent these secrets are from, bring with it apprehension and hesitation.

Some families certified with the agency have come through specifically to be certified for these AB 12 youth, wanting to be that mentor who can be there when the youth has questions, needs a place to stay, but also still giving space for building the ability of independence. It will be some years to come to be able to determine the success, or failure, of AB 12's impact in the long run as the bill is still in its beginning stages. However, it is a step in the right direction.

As can be seen, permanency plans require thought, planning, and challenging obstacles to overcome along the way for all parties involved. It is a process that many have no clue to the complexity of the discussion that go on in open and behind closed doors. What it ultimately comes down to, these are lives that are being juggled around, and we can only hope we are

constantly making the right choices in the long run.

3

Adoption world v. Foster Care world

Although you would think that there is little separation between the foster care world and the adoption world, that is not entirely the case. Because I have the experience of both worlds, I have been able to directly experience the differences, both within my agency and within the foster care and adoption community at large. There are so many rules and complexities involved in each world, that it is easy to see how they become separated as two distinctly different worlds.

From a county perspective, many county social workers in the reunification unit or permanency unit have little knowledge of the know-how in the adoption process and vice versa. Whenever there had been questions surrounding adoption, the active social worker would "get back to" us when they found out from a person who had more experience in that arena. Amusingly, I had an experience where an adoption social worker had to ask a co-worker in one of the other two units because the adoption social worker's specialty was adoptions issues. There are often comments made that it is uncertain why some workers in one unit do not know the specifics that go on in other units, as if the less they know, the better.

The agency I have worked for in these past nine years also has this separation between the two worlds. Even after transferring back to a foster care social worker, I was still one of the go-to people on issues and the process of adoption. Even though adoption has become a driving force in the past few years, more so than ever in my opinion, there is still that lack of knowledge that abounds. I have been a part of trainings for staff and foster parents regarding adoption for years. I often repeat topics and facts in these trainings yet I am often approached later to clarify, explain further, or give examples. From my experience, I have come to realize, if you have not been knee deep in the adoption world and the foster care world together, you will not know the differences and similarities. No matter how many times I try to teach people these small details, there will always be questions and a lack of know-how. Because of this, there will always be a divide between the worlds until they overlap and work together cohesively.

In an effort to bring these worlds closer, or at least parallel to one another, a new approach at my agency began a few years ago. This new approach is called concurrent planning. The purpose of concurrent planning is to limit placement changes as much as possible. And that is a great concept,…..in theory anyway.

A concurrent foster family becomes certified as a fost/adopt family, which means if the option of adoption arises, the family is ready to move forward as smoothly and quickly as possible with this plan. The goal is for a child or youth to be placed in a concurrent home with the initial plan of reunification as the main goal. However, if this plan falls through the cracks, plan B is already in place. Plan B with the foster family would be a permanent plan with the child or youth, in order of preference, by means of adoption, guardianship, or long term care. By following the concurrent process, it eliminates further placement changes…..in theory.

Although this can be a successful plan, this has not always been the case. Some people continue to come through the foster care process solely to be long term or short term foster parents, to "make a difference" in a child or youth's life, or "help a child in need." I hear those two quite often. With the push for concurrent foster families, even though long term care is an option, it is highly frowned upon. Most counties, from my experience, push adoption from the get go. There have been situations where adoption is not the best option, or if it is, it is not the best option right now.

From the other side, fost/adopt parents come through to be certified specifically for adoption. This becomes complicated when the child or children are in reunification. Some people come through and say, I want a low risk case. A low risk case usually means there is a less likelihood that the child would reunify with the birth parents or extended family members have not been identified. Adoption usually becomes the plan. A high risk case is when the child is likely to reunify with the birth parents or a relative has been identified and is in the process of being assessed for placement. The child would be a temporary placement. The problem is, no one can determine if a case is low risk or high risk. This can change in a drop of a hat. I always tell my families never to assume a case is one way or the other. I have had county placement workers tell families a case is low risk when within a couple of weeks this is in no way the case. In foster care and adoption, expect the unexpected, but hope for the best.

When We Fail with an Adoption Plan

There are circumstances where an adoption plan is not appropriate, or should be delayed. When I can see an adoption possibly becoming a failure, I put the breaks on any way I can. Adoption is not always the best option.

As I've said before, some people become foster parents to make a difference in a child or youth's life, as a foster parent, not an adoptive parent. Because of the rise of counties almost requiring a foster family to be a concurrent family before placement will occur, this sets up many families, as well as children, for challenges and possibly heart break in the not too distant future.

Let's imagine this scenario. A foster family accepts a placement of a child who is on a plan of family reunification. The reunification plan has been going very well, and the child was expected to reunify with the birth family within a few months, pending the birth family continues to show progress and follow the reunification plan. Somewhere along the line, the birth family falters and proceeded to fail their reunification plan. Another permanency plan begins to be discussed. Initially the first option is asking the foster family to adopt. But wait a minute! The family had no intention of really adopting because they were expecting the child to return to the birth family as was the initial plan. Often the county will begin to pressure the foster family in to adopting, using threats such as if the family does not adopt, the child will have to be moved from their care. First of all, the goal was to minimize moves. Not begin to make more moves if the foster parents' don't cave to the threats. Problem is, some counties will actually move a child to another home that are willing to begin a plan of adoption from the get-go, even if the child and previous foster family had bonded together.

I had a case where there were several siblings living in one foster home, moved there specifically so all of the siblings could be together, when the reunification plan failed. The foster parents began to get pressured to adopt the children. The foster parents were willing to adopt, some day, if the fit and circumstances were right. However, the family was not willing to adopt as at least two of the children did not want to be adopted, and were old enough to choose not to be adopted. The children were also still loyal to their birth mother. The foster parents were regularly expressing their frustrations with me on a regular basis, and, I for one agreed, adoption was not appropriate right now. Although I should not be sharing this, I did inform the foster parents to stand their ground and not be pressured in to any decision. The foster parents agreed and said if the county felt the need to move the children to find an adoption home, the family would assist with this transition.

The most frustrating part of this experience, after coming from adoptions back to foster care, a county adoption social worker used the threat and guilt trip on me. In the sweetest voice possible, the adoption social worker said if the parents were not willing to adopt the children, the county would have to seek out another home. The foster parents and I called the bluff. Let's get real, how easy is it going to be for a county to find what would likely be at least two separate homes, thus separating the children again, solely so the younger children can be adopted by some family some day, when the older children did not want to be adopted? To put this more in perspective, there were six children in this sibling set. Imagine separating six siblings from each other just so some of them can be adopted, whether they wanted to be or not. It was a risky chance, but calling the bluff worked. Why? Because it is very difficult to find a foster home that can take six children at once, for regulation and capacity sake as well as sure sanity. Six children ain't no easy feat, and add the "foster" issues, and you have a bag of exciting challenges. The county backed off and the children continue to live in the home together.

Another scenario that I have come across more frequently as of late is when adoption is being pushed to occur when the child or children are exhibiting some very challenging behaviors. Yes, when a fost/adopt parent comes in to the adoption and foster care processes, it is assumed he or she can handle a child on his or her own, thus becoming the identified parent for the child in the long run, without further supports and professionals involved. However, children from foster care, even those with minimalist behaviors, come with an extra degree of uncertainty. Down the road, years later, an adoptive child can begin to struggle, whether directly related to being adopted, or indirectly related to the foster care experience and the reason for removal from the birth family. Then there are those children whose behaviors begin to skyrocket as the adoption plan continues to be discussed and followed. In one such scenario, a very young boy who was in an active plan to be adopted with a sibling became physically aggressive towards a family pet to an extreme. The boy required constant supervision from then on around the family pet, unsure if the next time the animal would be beaten to death, literally. Wouldn't any parent have second thoughts under similar circumstances? But the county apparently did not find the situation serious enough to postpone an adoption until further services were provided. I find that concerning on many levels.

Although I am uncertain why the behaviors escalated in the child mentioned above, I have directly and indirectly experienced children in the adoption process whose negative behaviors increase around the topic of adoption. Adoption itself can be very apprehensive, just as much for an adult as for a child. Once the plan of adoption was taken off of the table in one case, the child's behavior stabilized. Adoption can do funny things to people. It can be a great thing, but it also always has an element of stress and trauma of its own.

Another scenario that may not be appropriate with adoption as the final outcome is for those children with severe special needs, such as autism, cerebral palsy, paralysis, and other such conditions which can require long term, hands on care. This in no way means that children with these needs can not, or should not be adopted, but there is a realistic understanding that this is a very difficult population of children that requires a much higher degree of dedication, commitment, patience, and experience. Children with severe special needs should be adopted when there is already regional center involvement established before finalization occurs. Just a recommendation on my part.

The Long Term Plan Fail

We are at a stage today that says no one, regardless of age, is unadoptable. Unfortunately, there are still youth emancipating out of the system or moving on to AB 12 as adults rather than being placed in a more positive permanent plan. Yes, we have failed some youth who probably should have been adopted or ended in a legal guardianship situation with a family member. Once a youth is in long term foster care, or permanent placement, the youth tends to be lost on the wayside. Settle in to that long term foster care placement, and work their way to the end of the program. Just another area where the "system" has failed. I know youth who were in long term care for 10 plus years because a more permanent plan was never made or even discussed. Ultimately, we may never know if some of those youth would have benefited from a more permanent plan outside of the "system."

Although, yes there are some youth that strive better without that permanent commitment, others struggle when leaving the system with no permanent bond to keep them afloat. There have been youth who have said they wished they had been adopted, but because they were older, or "difficult", an adoption plan was never discussed. Adoption or legal guardianship should be discussed as an option every six months to a year, regardless of the child's placement in long term foster care or not. It is honestly best practice. And if the youth does not want to be adopted or placed in guardianship, that should be discussed at length with the youth.

I have worked with families who have asked if a child in long term placement is adoptable. Yes, every child is adoptable. Just because they are not currently on an adoption track, due to behavior, family circumstances, whatever, does not mean the child or youth can never be on an adoption plan. Ultimately, the goal is to get children and youth out of the "system," but only at an appropriate time and with the appropriate plan.

4

Agency Social Workers

I am what you would identify as an agency social worker. For those children placed with a foster care agency or foster family agency (FFA), there will be at least two social workers involved: the county social worker and the agency social worker. The agency social worker will be the responsible party on behalf of the county social worker. The agency social worker ensures the child or children are being properly cared for by the foster family certified with the agency social worker's agency, and report to the county social worker. The agency social worker is usually the mediator between the county social worker and the foster parent or foster family. Foster agencies in themselves are also different, and follow their own set of rules that are aligned with Community Care Licensing (we will get to them at a later chapter). The type of support depends on the type of children the agency receives. Some agencies only require bi-weekly visitation by the agency social worker, and others require once a month visitation. The agency I have worked for requires weekly visitation with the social workers, unless other circumstances allow for reduced visitation to bi-weekly. The reason for a high engagement ratio is due to the fact that the agency I have worked for is considered a treatment foster care agency. This means our agency can receive extra supports and funding through the county to provide a higher level of supports and services to specific children, and their foster parents, that have been identified as demonstrating more challenging behaviors.

From a personal standpoint, being an agency social worker definitely has its perks, above and beyond those of a county social worker. As an agency social worker, I am not held obligated to the birth family, like those county workers in family maintenance and family reunification plans. I am not held to the child, and only the child, as some county workers are. I am not obligated to our foster parents only either. I can have an opinion, albeit a quiet one, without the need to choose one side over the other. My two top priorities are supporting the foster parents, and supporting and protecting the foster child. Unfortunately, sometimes this does require "taking sides."

Although foster parents and foster children should hold an element of restraint with their agency social worker, as with other professionals involved, I give my foster parents and foster children power. I offer myself up as the sounding board. If the family or children want to rant or vent, in private, I allow them that power. By doing so, I give them the space, a safe space, to express their frustrations, there lack of understanding, their roller coaster emotions, with a supportive space to do this.

Let's get real. Foster children did not ask to be removed from their family's care, did not ask to be put in a strange place, with strange people, with strange rules. Foster parents come in to this process to help out children, not knowing what they are really signing up for either. Given rules that at times appear ridiculous and extreme. And although we encourage foster parents to speak to other foster parents to get support from those experiencing similar situations, having a social worker who knows the "whys" of the system, even if we do not agree with them either, can be more supportive through a very challenging experience.

Truth be told, some agency social workers get positively frustrated with the process and rules at times too. The only difference is, we are being paid to follow those rules, and truthfully, usually there are reasons behind the rules. When I get to the section regarding Community Care Licensing, I will discuss this further.

As with all professionals involved with the foster care system, there are agency social workers that fall in the usual categories: the good, the bad, and the ugly.

The Good

Yes, there are still remarkable social workers in the world today. In fact, I know of at least a handful of agency social workers I would like to refer to as phenomenal, even after several years in the field. So the question is what makes for a good agency social worker, and, on that point, a phenomenal agency social worker?

Well, let's start with what makes a good agency social worker. As a social worker, there are multiple parties involved, even at the basic level. Let's take a simple scenario. The agency social worker communicates and interacts with a county social worker (primarily by phone, with the occasional in-person contact), the foster parent(s), and the foster child or children. A good social worker is able to make at least one good connection with a minimum of one of these parties. If a social worker has at least one good connection in this scenario, there is room for stability and progress.

I have had cases where I have had good rapport with the county social worker and the foster parents. I have had cases where I was able to build good rapport with the foster family and the foster child. I honestly believe if the foster parents are well committed to the child, then my rapport with the child is not altogether necessary. After all, some foster children have aversions towards any type of professionals connected to the "system." But can you blame them?

Another quality of a good social worker is action. When a foster parent or foster child requests or requires extra services, how quickly the social worker responds to this need is a key factor. Occasionally, a social worker must get pushy with county social workers, repeatedly requesting services or assistance on behalf of the foster child or children. And yes, occasionally "pushy" is the direction an agency social worker has to take.

One of the things synonymous with a social worker is paperwork. Mounds and mounds of paperwork. A good social worker is able to generally keep up on the paperwork, the reports, the deadlines. I say generally because during times of high caseloads and crisis moments, staying current on the paperwork can be unrealistic (unless you want to work 60-70 hours a week instead of just 40-50 hours a week). A normal caseload at my agency is a high of 15 children per social worker.

Another great quality of a good social worker is being able to identify when he or she is not demonstrating the progress that a social worker could be making, whether with the foster parent or child. If there is a problem within the relationship between the foster parent and the social worker, the child or youth are going to be able to see or feel this distance, and may use that to his or her advantage. Working with a diverse population, both the foster parent population and the foster child population, is a juggling act.

43

And one that should always be monitored and assessed for an appropriate match. If there is not a match or connection, roadblocks go up. A good social worker is able to identify these roadblocks, and will step up and address this, either one on one with the foster parent, or with the social worker's supervisor. A change in workers may need to occur for a healthier, progressive change.

I was struggling with my approach and relationship with a difficult child in one of my foster homes. I spoke with the foster mother that maybe the child would progress more if I stepped out of the picture and allowed another social worker to step in. Unfortunately (or fortunately), the foster mother refused my proposal, saying SHE required my support. This was one of those few cases where my relationship and connection with my foster parent was stronger than with the child, but by being as supportive as I was to the foster parent, she was able to continue to provide care for a very difficult child much longer than was expected.

One of the perks of being a social worker in the current age is cell phones. Without them, some matters could reach crisis mode without an opportunity of distinguishing the fires. With cell phones, agency social workers are easy to contact with a reasonable turnaround time of a call back. This can easily nip a problem issue in the bud before it reaches an escalated point. It allows for another easy means for venting for foster parents and foster youth alike. One downfall to the cell phone is some agency social workers will answer their phones after hours or on weekends, though this is not a requirement. A good social worker might answer calls while a phenomenal social worker will play it smart by screening the calls and determining if the issue is worth handling now or at a later, more appropriate time. Some social workers prefer to be the point of contact at all times because they know their cases, they know the issues, they know what may and may not work.

Speaking of the phenomenal agency social worker, this person can maintain excellent relationships with most parties involved, across the board. The social worker has compassion, tolerance, patience, and, above all else, professionalism at all times. A crisis can arise at any time, and you won't even see this person break a sweat (even if internally he or she is). The phenomenal worker not only gets the job at hand done, they go above and beyond on occasions, and make the whole process look smooth as silk. Having the ability to remain that dedicated and professional after years and years in the field is remarkable, and a gift. These people make the business worth fighting for.

The Bad (or Not-so-good)

So every professional arena has workers that are not as up to par as they could, or should, be. A bad agency social worker does not necessarily make the person a horrible social worker, just not good in some respects. A bad social worker still attempts to try to do good at some point in the game.

A bad agency social worker is the one that does not get involved one way or the other. A foster child is terrorizing the foster parent, the foster parent reports it to the social worker, and the social worker does not do anything. Is it because the social worker is not reading the communication right? Does the social worker not know how to respond? A good social worker would at least acknowledge the behavior, acknowledge the foster parents efforts (or attempts at an effort), and make suggestions on how to respond. Or even respond with "Let me see what I can find to help us with this situation." A social worker needs to be able to read between the lines and determine if the cry for help is legitimate or just a means of venting frustrations.

A bad social worker does not answer phone calls regularly, or does not respond back in a timely manner to phone messages or emails. When a foster parent asks or requests help, this social worker does not respond in a timely manner or with any suggestions that prove fruitful. Paperwork is not always complete, done in a timely manner (even when time allows for it to be), or completed appropriately.

Although working with a bad agency social worker can be tolerable, and can get the basic job done, a good social worker would always be the ultimate goal. However, a bad social worker certainly beats out the ugly agency social worker any time.

The Ugly

Obviously there is a difference between the bad and the ugly agency social worker. The ugly social worker is the one here for the money. Sadly, social workers do not make enough financially for the work they do and the stress they endure, but this worker does as minimal as possible for that paycheck. Relationships are unprofessional with at least one party if not several involved in a case, or across several cases. There have been moments when a foster parent will actually "fire" their agency social worker because he or she did not feel their needs were being met or there was insufficient support offered. Truthfully, even a good social worker can get "fired" from their foster parent, but that's another story.

Another huge issue from the ugly agency social worker is when personal bias and personal opinion gets in the way of doing the job appropriately. For example, an agency social worker clashes with a foster parent and the child suffers for the tension. An ugly social worker will continue to engage in the tense and inappropriate relationship rather than requesting to be moved off the case, thereby prolonging further problems and issues, or blaming the foster parent or foster child for the "problems."

Although people who suffer from mental illness should be allowed to work and make the most of a productive life, there is a point when mental illness can be a serious problem. A staff member was briefly employed with the agency who appeared, for all intensive purposes, qualified and a well balanced individual. However, after a mental outburst in the agency's office, (luckily when only staff and not clients were within the vicinity) it was determined the staff member could no longer provide services for our foster children while in the current state. The staff left the agency, hopefully to take care of the issues at hand. Something to keep in mind is, although there is a myth and poor assumption that individuals who work in the mental health and social services fields are of perfect mental and emotional states, this is in no way the truth. Every human being has equal opportunity of being affected, directly and indirectly, by mental health issues. A big concern with this though is that a person suffering from mental health issues that is not getting appropriate care and treatment could be detrimental to the care and well being of a foster child. This must be carefully monitored.

Foster care is a complex, challenging arena, and a foster parent needs support through this process. Having a good agency social worker is paramount to the success and well being of a productive, healthy experience through this process.

5

County Social Workers

Before I begin, I must put a disclaimer out there regarding county social workers. Most often, county social workers are over worked with high caseloads, ranging from 45 to 60 children. This becomes more of a challenge for those counties that have begun to require monthly visits for all the children on their caseload. I honestly do not know the specific requirements of time past, but I had worked with a foster youth who was a part of the adoption track, who really should not have been for five plus years, who was visited maybe once or twice a year by the county worker. If a child appeared stable in placement, visits appeared not to be mandatory, or if they were, not all of the county workers were following the rules.

Around 2013 or so, counties required FFA workers to complete a new document for them, called an SOC 160, which documented the FFA worker's visit with the child. Several counties relied on these documents as the documents could cover any visit the county worker would have been required to make. However, this was utilized only on a county-by-county basis. Although a few counties required the document from the FFA, and some used these forms in lieu of visiting the child themselves, there was a requirement for the county worker to still visit the child in person an average of once a month. Imagine visiting 45 to 60 children once a month, on top of the other paperwork, reports, appointments, scheduling of services, court appearances, and other necessities. Another thing to keep in mind, the county social workers are not just involved with the foster child and/or foster families. The majority of county social workers, especially those in family reunification and long term foster care maintain contact, support, and services to the birth family as well. This can include setting up visits with extended family members, determining if there are extended family members out of the area (even out of state) that may be a more appropriate placement setting for the foster child, and many other potential tasks. There are many factors involved in being a county social worker, but even these professionals have their set of incompetent workers.

The Effective Worker

Be blessed if you manage to meet or work with an effective county social worker. Although they do exist, they seem few and far between. A truly effective county worker is able to juggle the caseload well, both the foster children and the birth families alike. This individual knows much, if not most, of the details of the case and history, and is aware of what services or techniques may work well for the child. Referrals are made without question or hesitation, the job gets done, and results come quickly. This worker responds back quickly and timely, or regularly answers the phone when called.

I have worked with several effective county workers over the years, and I feel truly honored to have had the opportunity to work with them. There is no one county that is better than another, so the effective workers are scattered. I have noticed there appear to be stronger workers in the long term placement units, a few in the adoption units, and county workers who are new to their job. Nothing like a go-getter from the beginning, those who have not had time to lose their spark. There are good county workers in the reunification unit, but these workers are harder to judge as their goal is generally different than the foster families, sometimes the agencies, and even other professionals involved. Most county social workers are at least generally effective at what they do, thank goodness. However, there are those baskets of bad eggs too.

Ineffective Worker

I have heard an increase in stories from my co-workers over the past year of the most ineffective county social workers. These are the workers that come with the horror stories. Some of them should have retired years ago (and still have not), or some of them should have been fired (but have not). The worst part is when the county social worker has an agenda, and the rest of the parties involved, including the child, birth family, and foster parent, have no idea what the agenda is, or if they do, have no idea where it came from.

The worker that tells you one thing in the moment, then will turn around and tell you a completely different thing in the next. Or the one who flat out denies ever saying something to begin with even it was very obvious he or she did, because where the heck else did that come from?

The ineffective county social worker who seems to have no clue what is going on, even though they really should. The one that cannot answer the judge because he or she has not been doing their job.

And then there is the county social worker with a personal agenda. For whatever reason, the county worker wants the birth parents to fail, or cannot stand the foster parents.

I always tell my foster parents be kind to the county social worker, but if there is ever a serious problem with a county worker, come to the agency social worker first. Do not ever try to go directly to the county social worker yourself, as they may take the defense and the foster parent has just lost the county worker as an ally. You never want to lose the county worker as an ally, even if you do not agree with their plan or the way they do things. Always try to maintain a neutral relationship with the county worker if there is a problem. Always come across for the child's best interest. If connecting with the child's attorney or the county worker's supervisor is inevitable, do whatever you can not to burn that bridge. A county worker can be your best ally through the process or your worst nightmare.

Professional Courtesy Wanted

Amusingly, some county social workers will place with the agency, knowing there is an agency social worker involved, yet will manage to avoid some contacts with the agency worker. I usually put a disclaimer out for our foster parents, especially the newer parents coming through the process to become certified, that calling a county worker directly is a no-no. County social workers have plenty on their plates, not needing a frustrated foster parent calling a couple of times a day, asking about the case, asking about visits, asking about most anything. If a county social worker calls a foster parent directly, I encourage the foster parent to return the call, but with caution. Some county social workers go directly to the foster parent to avoid any additional phone calls, such as when setting times and days for visitations. However, keeping the county worker on the phone for more than what was asked for can burn that bridge quickly.

There are those workers that go directly to the foster parent, rather than anyone else from the foster care agency, for placements. Some county social workers do build good relationships with the foster parents, and by doing so are aware of the foster parent's strengths and weaknesses. Although relationships with the county are strongly encouraged, everyone can do with some good PR, there is a reason there is a mediator, agency social worker, involved.

Once a foster parent has built a relationship with the county social worker, I encourage the foster parent to continue to be the direct point of contact. If any challenges arise, I recommend giving back the responsibility of the point of contact person to the agency social worker. One positive piece about county workers who contact foster parents directly is there is less chances for miscommunication. A negative piece is the foster parents may sound like they are complaining or inflexible.

Ultimately, every foster parent will have contact in some way or another with a county worker during a placement. If you become a foster parent directly through the county, the county worker is really your only obvious support and point of contact through the process. The experience with the county worker will depend on how good of a county worker the individual is as well as the foster parent's ability to be flexible, understanding, and to some point, professional.

I recently heard from a co-worker who has a family member who is employed through the county that county social workers do not have respect for FFAs and their workers. True, some workers and FFAs are not professional, ethical, or moral, but the reality is FFAs are necessary. A county social worker needs FFAs to keep their jobs. An FFA needs foster children and county social workers to exist. In the end, we need each other, whether we like it or not.

6

Court-related Professionals

Obviously because the child welfare system is involved, there will be court-related professionals involved on different levels. Court hearings are held, on average, of every six months on any given case. Of course, hearings can be delayed or postponed, which would then throw off the six month timeline, but that's the gist. As a foster care social worker, I have had little contact with most court-related professionals. As an adoption social worker, I had more involvement with judges, on a positive level. The three most common court-related professionals that are usually involved in a case are judges, children's attorneys, birth parents' attorneys, and CASA workers. Although CASA workers are not specifically held to the court systems as, say, the attorney, since they have court in their title, and they are assigned by requesting them from the court system, CASA workers will be included here.

Judges

I do not know about the rest of you, but even under the best circumstances, judges have always scared me to death. These individuals who sit up on their high benches, who can literally make or break a case by any given decision, have quite the power in their hands. They are given information from attorneys and county social workers, are expected to make an impartial decision on what he or she believes is in the child or children's best interest, and is usually only based on a piece of the picture. Occasionally, foster parents attend the hearings and can have their voices heard. Other times they are only seen, not heard.

Although the attorneys and county social workers can, and do, make recommendations on the cases, the judge ultimately can make whatever decision he or she chooses. I had heard of a case from a co-worker where the judge made a decision that was completely out of left field. No one was recommending what the judge decided, and ultimately the judge has the power to make any decision, without clarification or reasoning.

Children 10 years an older are generally required to attend the hearings, unless it would be detrimental for them, but can also choose not to be present. Younger children are usually not required to attend hearings, but can.

As an adoption social worker, I met several different judges, more than I likely would have as a foster care social worker. The majority of the occasions where I was in contact with a judge, though, were usually at the end phase during the finalization. The truth be told, several judges enjoy these little happy moments out of long days of challenging cases. A family is becoming permanent, and they get to be party to this. After the first dozen or so finalizations, going in to a court room, in front of a judge and bailiff, was like walking in to any other place of business. Only difference was most parties were in their best attire. Easy as pie!

Judges truly do have a difficult job. They are the sole person making a decision for a child or children that will inevitably impact that child or children for the rest of their lives within the span of as little as a few minutes. That is an awesome, scary power to have!

Attorneys

Amusingly, I have met maybe three or four attorneys of foster children I have worked with in my nine years. I have met only a couple of birth parents' attorney, mainly through attending a court proceeding. Otherwise, little involvement occurs with the attorney from the FFA level.

One of the three memorable experiences I have had was not altogether a positive one. The foster parent requested for the attorney to be present in an attempt for him to be another voice during a struggling school issue for one child. The attorney attended an IEP (Individualized Education Plan), but sat on the outskirts of the main group and said next to nothing, with the exception of identifying who he was. He never attended another school meeting, and there were plenty regarding the child I am discussing. However, his absence did not affect the process one way or another.

A second experience involved me dropping off children to visit with their attorney, so I had minimal contact other than a greeting at introduction and a greeting at the finish. The attorney met with the older children for about five to ten minutes, then met with all three youngest children for five minutes together. I cannot honestly make any sort of impression based on this contact though did find it odd that after traveling for 30 minutes with six kids in the car, the children met with the attorney for a total of 15 to 20 minutes.

My third memorable experience with an attorney was when the attorney came to the foster home to talk one on one with the child. The attorney was, shall we say, a bit aggressive almost towards the foster mother. Maybe I was over analyzing this, and maybe he was direct and to the point, as attorneys have little time to do many things. The one positive revelation I had from this experience was the true commitment I observed from the attorney's interaction with the foster youth. This attorney truly made an effort for this client. I heard rumors from other co-workers that even though this attorney can be difficult to work with at times, he did attempt to do what was best for his clients. Ultimately, that is what we ask, and hope, for.

One thing to remember is, an attorney is ultimately looking out for the best interest of the child. The child's attorney does not automatically side with the birth parents' attorney, as some people have speculated. In fact, there have been circumstances where the birth parents' and child's attorney have clashed over case recommendations.

A recent case brings me to this point. Although I was not the direct social worker on the case, I listened to the frustrating occurrences on an on going basis. Four children had been in foster care for a year longer than should have occurred. Two relatives, on separate sides of the family, came forward to try to get custody of the children. Without going in to specifics, the whole case was complicated and, to put it mildly, a hot mess. One relative was ready to take the children, but for some reason the process of assessing the relative fell through the cracks, and no one bothered following up with the process. In the meantime, a second relative, on the other side of the family, came forward and was close to finishing the assessment process when things ground to a halt. From my perspective, this situation dragged on for no apparent reason other than the birth parents were suddenly arguing over which relative should be able to take the children. One thing that makes all of this complicated was the fact the birth parents were technically still together, even though they were not supposed to, and were disagreeing over where the children should go. What made the situation more complicated was the fact that the birth parents were already deemed not appropriate for the children to return to their care, because they were together when instructed not to be. The attorneys for the children and birth parents were fighting in court over where the children should go. Truthfully, the children should never have been in the system as long as they were. I hold the birth parents and the system solely responsible for that mess. Those children deserved better.

CASA workers

A CASA worker, or Court Appointed Special Advocates, is an individual who volunteers his or her services to a case. The CASA worker is a support person for the child. Usually children who are demonstrating difficult behaviors have a CASA worker requested by the county social worker or attorney through the judge. The positive part of having a CASA worker involved is the fact they are not technically a "part of the system." These individuals are truly there for the benefit and support of the child. A CASA worker usually must complete an intensive training before being able to become a CASA worker.

I have learned that a CASA worker can be an angel sent from heaven or a mischief maker brought to cause chaos. A CASA worker actually can have a lot of power in a foster care case.

I have heard at least two negative stories where a CASA worker was involved. Two girls were in the process of being adopted. The foster parents came through to become foster parents specifically to adopt these girls, who had previously lived with the foster mother's sister who was a certified foster parent. The foster child had difficult behaviors (one had a unique eating disorder and the other had some behavioral issues), but the foster parents were committed to adopting them. The adoption was delayed, and was almost dropped altogether because of the interference of the CASA worker.

A second case ended with a foster child being moved from a foster home because the CASA worker did not want the child to remain in the foster home. I understand if the purpose was for safety reasons, but it came out later that the CASA worker simply did not like the foster parent.

Although the two experiences I have had, mainly through second hand experience, were negative, I still believe in the need and power of a CASA worker. The ultimate goal is to be a support for foster children yet are not tagged as "part of the system." There are benefits as well as pitfalls to having a CASA worker involved, but ultimately, the child's best interest should always be at the forefront.

7

Other professionals

In the situations where the child is having a difficult time adjusting to placement moves or other reasons for increasing behavioral outbursts, other professionals become involved. There are situations where minor concerns can result in the involvement in additional professionals. The most common professional involved in foster care cases is a therapist. But there are other programs and resources available to children in foster care. Some of the support services are also available for children in general such as therapy, Wrap services, TBS services, and regional center services.

Therapy

Therapy comes in all forms and sizes, so to speak. Foster children can be involved in individual therapy, group therapy, family therapy, or workshop-type groups. I include workshop-type groups because these can be skill building groups that are less therapeutic, and more about teaching

and practices. For example, a skill building workshop for improving social

skills is not altogether therapeutic, but probably necessary and best learned

in a group setting.

The problem with therapists in the foster care world, and even more so

in the adoption world, is the fact there are therapists who work with foster

and adopted children who really do not have a clue of what a child

experiences through these situations. I'm sorry, but a therapist who works

with children who have a two parent family (both birth parents) with minor

behavioral issues is not going to know how to work with a child from a

foster family who has moved multiple times, seen traumas that most adults

have not experienced, and understanding where the behaviors and

emotions are coming from. True, children in foster care experience many

of the same situations and circumstances as a "normal" child (really, what is

"normal?"), but compound that with so many other variables and

experiences brought on from the foster care experience itself.

I have met all types of therapists. The ones that know it all, the ones

that do not get involved, the ones that are never available, the ones that are

always available, the ones that are experienced and really do know what they

are doing, and the ones who should not be on a case at all, for whatever

reason.

I have worked with foster children who refuse to go to their therapy sessions because "we don't do anything" or "it isn't helping anyway." Even though many of these children who are refusing actually need therapy, the problem is they need a good therapist. Good therapists are hard to come by, and then you throw in the obstacle of the foster care piece. If therapy is not working, take a break and try again. Or advocate for a change in therapist.

There is one area I must address: play therapy. At the simple mention of this form of therapy, most people, especially foster parents that I have worked with, cringe. Some people say it's useless, the children are not getting anything from it, the children are only playing and how is that therapy, and so on. Let's get realistic for a moment. First of all, imagine any child five years or younger that is developmentally on target for his or her age, and imagine him or her trying to talk about their feelings. Any child does not really understand the true ramifications of emotions, their meanings, or how to discuss them. How do you expect to get a young child, one who has seen some pretty traumatic things in his or her life that even adults have a difficult time finding the words to express and/or explain, and are nowhere near being developmentally on target for their age? Play therapy can be a phenomenal way for a therapist to get to the roots of emotions and trauma with a child who does not have the language development, or comprehension level, to understand the traumatic experience. Does that mean all therapists that attempt to use play therapy know what they are doing or how to use the play therapy to a productive standpoint? No. But all I ask is that people give play therapy a chance, because "typical talk therapy" does not and will not work for young children, especially children from the foster care system.

TBS

Although Therapeutic Behavioral Services (TBS) have been around for a minimum of a decade, it appears to be the new big thing again. I was a worker in the TBS program back in 2001 through 2004 at another foster care and adoption agency. It was "new" back then, but it appears to have picked up steam again in last two years or so. The purpose of TBS is to get in, work the problem, and get out in a relatively short period of time.

A child is referred to TBS services if he or she has already been hospitalized at a psychiatric facility or is at risk of losing their placement. TBS is not just for foster children, but also children living in the birth family as well. Foster children have a stronger chance of getting referred to the services since they are already considered in out-of-home care. Most counties try to refer to TBS before they will consider other services or resources. TBS services are assessed every 30 days, or more frequently as needed, but can last up to either a year or year and a half.

I have worked both as a TBS worker, in the past, and with a TBS team for foster youth I was working with as a social worker. I give this program kudos. This team has a difficult task handed to them, have a short intense amount of time spent with these children, and are expected to produce results. If a child cannot benefit from TBS, the next step is usually a group home or residential treatment environment. Like a police officer, a TBS worker gets involved with children on their worst days. Bless their hearts! TBS usually comes as a small team of two or three people per case, at least this is true of the TBS program that works in our agency. The Behavioral Specialist is the one-one-one person who works directly with the child in the situation, in the environment, for up to several hours a day, a few days a week. In the beginning, the time is intense and rapidly decreases. This person is there to observe the behaviors in their original environment. The individual teaches new routines, new coping skills, and general new skills within the moment. Occasionally there are two different Behavioral Specialists working with one child, depending on circumstances.

A second team member oversees the Behavioral Specialist who is called the Clinical Behavioral Analyst. This person usually sets up and runs the monthly review meetings, meets with the caregiver, and also occasionally meets one-on-one with the child. TBS can work in familial settings as well if the problems and behaviors arise more frequently within the home among the family. The Clinical Behavioral Analyst reports to the Clinical Program Manager, who for all intensive purposes is the supervisor overseeing all staff. Although the supervisor is more often involved in the managerial aspects of the program, this person can cover for other staff as needed.

WRAP services

Wrap services pretty much is what it sounds like. Provide multiple supports and services, and wrap the family in resources for a chance of success. Wrap services have some similarities to TBS in that referrals occur when a child is at risk of losing their placement. Wrap services can be requested prior to a child possibly losing their placement or after a child has transitioned to a new placement, such as from a group home back to the birth home, or group home to a foster home.

The intent of Wrap services is to utilize a team to help assist and support a child or youth and the family in maintaining the family as a whole. The interesting piece about Wrap is it is focused on working with the family and child need, not what has worked for others. When it is said "individualized," Wrap utilizes this definition to the fullest. Just because there is a family belief system that appears dysfunctional or unrealistic to others on the team, it is up to the team to work within these beliefs and realities to keep the family together. The purpose of Wrap is not to bring skills or processes the family would not even bother utilizing in their home or even consider as an option. This is why this process works directly with the family, whether birth or foster.

Wrap services can be a short term process or a long term process. I have seen children receive Wrap services for a few years. There is no definitive timeline, other than reaching the goal at hand. With Wrap, services can range from the typical to the unusual. A birth parent may need help paying utility bills. A program is found for that. A family may need to find adequate childcare. A program or resources are found for that. A birth parent needs a refrigerator. A program is found for that. Usually the caregiver, whether a foster parent or birth parent, receives support from an individual known as a parent partner. It helps for the caregiver to have a support who is a neutral party and advocating on their behalf.

Regional Center

It's actually generally normal when a foster child younger than three years old is referred to a regional center. Most foster children are in some form or shape delayed, whether by a few months or more, due to neglect, lack of stimulation as a child, or not entering the school system until later than he or she should have. Regional centers are to assess and support children and adults who are developmentally and/or physically handicapped. Up to the age of three years old, children can receive some basic support services to help them reach their milestones and catch up developmentally.

There are cases of foster children who are chronologically 13 or 14 years old yet are developmentally at the age of six or seven years old. People tend to forget that this means you have a 13 or 14 year old, physically, looking you in the face, but he or she is thinking at a six or seven-year-old's mind frame and intellect. Some foster parents forget about the difference between chronological age (the actual age of the child) and the developmental age (what age the child or youth think's and functions at).

Most children who have regional services in place up to the age of three years old are assessed out of services. Unless there is a severe delay noticed in the three year old's assessment, services will be discontinued. I think the theory behind this is that children at a very young age, one to five years old, have growing brains, and this is the best time for learning.

If a child is assessed as developmentally delayed after the age of three years old, the child is usually determined to be a regional center client for life. However, there is a catch, which I will get to in a moment. First, some of the typical services that come from regional center support can include in one or more of the following services: speech therapy, occupational therapy, physical therapy, or for the younger children, a teacher. With the younger children, the service providers usually come to the foster home to provide care. When services are at the beginning and most intense stage, there are as many as three people working with the child up to three times a week. As the child progresses, services begin to taper off.

For children older than three years old who have been deemed appropriate to become a regional center client, having services provided while in foster care gets complicated, and at times frustrating. Because a child is in foster care, some regional centers will not provide services for the child, laying the responsibility of services on the FFA agency. I agree that there are some services that an FFA should initially be responsible for. However, services that require regional center services are usually above and beyond the ability of an FFA agency. Once a foster youth turns 18 years old, some services begin to kick in, such as adult day programs, adult activities and outings, seeking residential or other living options, and employment assistance. Some services do not begin until the person has turned 21 years old.

ITFC services

There are a few agencies, such as the one I have worked for, that provides a specific service to the children who are in foster homes within the agency. For children who have trouble following routine and structure, struggle at school with behaviors and/or academics, demonstrate poor peer skills, have poor hygiene, can be disruptive and argumentative with adults, and a variety of other disruptive behaviors, they can be referred to Intensive Treatment Foster Care Services (ITFC). This service is only provided for the children placed in the agency providing the services.

The children who qualify for ITFC meet weekly with their agency social worker, usually have a Family Specialist or Support Counselor working one-on-one with them, and are usually involved in some form of extra services or activities, such as equine therapy (horse therapy), anger management groups, individual or group therapy, specialized therapy (such as for sexual predators), or involvement in a regular extracurricular activity. I often say that ITFC is somewhat similar to TBS in that the goals are generally the same, some of the work and skill building are similar, and technically ITFC is supposed to be a short term service. Some counties are not as rigid with the parameters of ITFC as they are with TBS. This is in the process of changing, but the truth is ITFC services cost less than a group home which is where some of these children are heading if ITFC services had not been put in to place.

There are probably other services out there worth mentioning, but these are some of the typical services I have experience working with for foster children and adopted children. The truth of the matter is, probably half of the children in foster care will end up requiring some extra service at some point in time in their foster care experience, but the key to remember is, sometimes extra help and support can be a blessing.

8

Community Care Licensing

This chapter is mainly for those working with foster care agencies. The plus about being a foster parent certified through a county directly is you are not held to the same standards as foster parents through an FFA. Yes, county foster homes still have rules and regulations to follow, and the foster home must pass an inspection, but the rules are often grey rather than black and white, and the rules are fewer than with an FFA. FFA's are held accountable, to some degree, to the counties that are placing children with them, and to Community Care Licensing (CCL).

The sad truth is that CCL is the equivalent to the likes of judges. Without doing anything, simply by stepping in to the office, they bring on pure fear to everyone within the vicinity. Whenever CCL is in the office, co-workers notoriously have somewhere else they have to be. CCL truly gets a bad rep. But they do hold a power that is scary, and they can take down an agency as quick as the snap of the fingers. Their job, however, is for a good cause. CCL is the regulator of residential facilities across the board. This includes adult centers, adult group homes, foster care homes, youth group homes, and, I discovered recently, youth shelters.

Reasons behind the Rules

Many foster parents complain about some of the rules and regulations they have to follow to be a foster parent. Generally there is a realistic reason behind many of the rules that must be followed and all in the name of safety for the children. I will outline a few general rules and explain the basic reasoning behind a few of them. I have heard foster parents say, on numerous occasions, they do not understand why foster parents have to follow so many stringent rules when birth parents are held to the barest minimum. That is the unfair reality to foster care, unfortunately.

The swimming pool with a five foot fence around it, regardless of a child or youth's age, is necessary. Just because a child says they know how to swim, does not always mean they really do. Two children fell in to an un-gated swimming pool, on two separate occasions in two separate counties. One died by drowning, the other was permanently brain-dead. A frustrating, but realistic rule.

In our agency, children are to be checked for height and weight on a monthly basis. This actually comes from an incident where there was only county involvement who only visit once a month if you're lucky. A child was found underweight and malnourished because height and weight were not checked regularly. Another good reason for this is being able to determine if a child or youth has an eating disorder. The earlier its discovered, the earlier treatment and therapy can begin.

The rule on medication storage has changed over the years. With the new prudent parenting rule (which is an exceptionally gray area), medication no longer has to be locked up. In fact, I was told that we can not even advice or say that a lock box is a good idea, even though it is. Medication of all kinds used to be required to be locked up whether over the counter, prescription, or simple cough drops. That rule in itself brought in arguments of its own (what kind of lock box is appropriate, does it need a key lock or code lock, where am I allowed to put the box, etc). Ever since the introduction of the prudent parenting policy, what to do with the medication has been a scary topic. There is a reason to lock up medication obviously. We do not want a little one to get ahold of someone's pain medication. We do not need a teen that is suicidal or drug dependent to steal medication that could inevitably kill him or her.

There was a recent incident at our agency where a young child got ahold of a strong pain medication while at a babysitter's house. Under the prudent parenting rule, we do not regulate the homes of babysitters with the exception of background checks such as fingerprinting and driving records if the babysitter will be driving the child anywhere. The good news is the babysitter noticed in time before the child could swallow the pill. However, this brought with it a string of questions and concerns within our agency. Reasons like this are when you want a rule about locking up medication. The same can be said for the rule of what to do with making sharp objects, such as knives, inaccessible. A few of the things to consider in either of these cases is the children's ages, how likely are the children to attempt to reach the object, and what are the behavioral issues that may lead to a child trying to get ahold of such things.

Another rule I hear grumblings about regularly is the locking up of firearms and ammunition. The part that brings on the argument is that our rule says the gun and the ammunition must be locked up separately, and not in the same area. I understand that if a burglar breaks in, the homeowner probably would like to be able to have access to their firearm quickly, and have it armed at a moments notice. However, get real. Even parents who are not foster parents should re-think this. There have been plenty of situations in the news where a child got ahold of the family firearm and shot mom, dad, a sibling, or a friend.

Inspections of the home should be expected. I understand that some people have an issue with strangers looking in their refrigerators, closets, and under the beds, but there is truly a legitimate reason for this. Agency staff as well as counties must ensure that there is adequate food and the children at no time are ever starving or wanting for food. Closets are to be used for the children's belongings, not a storage space for the foster parents' junk. I'm sorry that's what storage units, other closet spaces, or garages are for. These children deserve to have their own space because they likely came from a situation where they did not have their own space or bed. Look under the beds? Absolutely! There was a situation early in my years at the agency where a crisis situation came up where a foster home was raided. The home was searched, while the poor foster children were still in the home early in the morning. Police discovered firearms hidden under an adult son's bed. Even the foster parents were oblivious to what their own child was hiding under their noses. The children were abruptly moved from what was going to be a forever home for them. It was truly a disturbing situation across the board.

Certain temperatures are necessary to monitor. One, the water temperature must be within a specific range so as not to scold a person. And trust me, this absolutely can happen in any home. There was a case of this at one of the other agency's sites after an adoption. A child can reach up and grab the water faucet in the blink of an eye and turn on the hot water to scold him or herself. By keeping the temperature within a certain range, this would be avoided even if the little one was mischievous for that split second. A home should be comfortable. This does not mean be cheap by not running the air conditioner when its 100 plus degrees outside. The same can be said during colder weather.

I must bring up prudent parenting. This new policy has been around for about two to three years, I believe. This is one of those few rules that is almost entirely in the gray area. Some rules are very black and white, like the water temperature must be within a certain range. When this policy came out, questions abounded. And for good reason. The purpose of prudent parenting is an effort to "normalize" the life of a foster child or youth. Instead of needing approvals for every little thing, such as staying the night at a friend's house for a slumber party without the need to fingerprint everyone in the friend's family, a foster parent can prudently decide whether or not their foster child can do such things. The thing our agency informs our families about this rule is to remember one thing, if CCL ever came in and questioned the foster parent for a decision he or she made under prudent parenting, the foster parent better have a realistic reason for their decision. If this were the foster parent's birth child, how would a decision have been made?

One more rule that must be discussed, even if only briefly, is foster children's personal rights. This is a big one. So many little pieces fall under this category. This is one of the bigger areas that agency foster parents receive complaints against their home. A foster child has many rights, and for good reason. The last thing our society needs is to bring more baggage to a foster child's life than what he or she has already experienced prior to removal. There are at least 26 identified personal rights afforded a foster child.

Here are just a few: right to feeling safe; right to choose to move from a foster home within reason; right to attend court hearings; right to call CCL whenever he or she chooses; the right to call the child's county social worker, agency social worker, or attorney when he or she chooses to; right to attend religious services of their choice even if not the same as the foster parent; right not to be restrained by a foster parent or other adult; "to be free of unreasonable searches of personal belongings" (this one frustrates parents); the right to participate in school and extracurricular activities; and so on.

There are other regulations and rules that might be worth exploring, but I will keep it simple for now. For our agency, the two most common complaint issues are lack of proper supervision and personal rights violations.

COA

There are a few agencies that not only abide by CCL rules and regulations, but also Council of Accreditation (COA) standards. The agency I have worked for also followed COA standards, which did sometimes cause more restrictions on what our agency and foster parents could do. One of the major restrictions is placement capacity. As a COA agency, our foster parents can not exceed the capacity of five children in the household without an approved exception on file. This includes all children living in the home, whether birth children, foster children, or other children that foster parent is raising for whatever reason. The one exception to this rule, which in itself is usually a rare case, is if the placement of foster siblings together is the only avenue. Most county agencies want siblings to remain together. In this day and age there are often referrals for sibling sets as large as seven to eight children. CCL has to approve an above capacity exception, and these exceptions are becoming more rare by the minute. There are many FFA agencies that choose not to be accredited by these standards.

The Complaint process

The complaint process is a very stressful time for all involved. The best that anyone can do is be patient, be optimistic, and ride it out.

There are two ways a complaint comes about. The most common, and most hopeful one, is if a child tells the agency social worker, or an agency staff member, the initial complaint. It is always good going in to a complaint process knowing what we are up against. The second way a complaint is made is from external sources, such as school personnel, therapists, CASA workers, coaches, church members, extended family members of the foster parent, birth parent, or anyone not directly connected to the FFA agency. Usually the agency may not even be aware of a complaint until CCL has come to the office to either open the complaint file or close one with the findings. Rather scary actually. The part that disturbs foster parents the most about the process is they often feel left out of the loop and unsupported. The problem is, as an agency, if anyone does speak with the foster parents about the complaint in any way, the agency can be fined. This impedes CCL's investigation and is a big no-no. Agency staff cannot say anything about the complaint. Staff try to remain as supportive as possible without overstepping the rule. In some cases, the foster parent may already know the complaint is pending (like if a foster child said the foster parent hit them in the foster parent's presence). In other cases, the foster parents do not know, in which case the agency social worker cannot even say there is a complaint against the home. Even if the foster parent is aware of the pending investigation, the agency staff cannot discuss the complaint in any fashion until the closing of the complaint.

What happens initially at the time of the complaint depends on the type of complaint. In some cases of a physical abuse complaint where there have been marks observed, the children can be immediately removed form the foster home, especially if they are young and nonverbal. In cases of reported abuse, if the child is of age and is able to make decisions for him or herself, the foster child can refuse to leave or be moved from the home. If the complaint is of a nature that does not put the child or children in danger, the child can remain in the home.

CCL comes to the agency office to open the complaint file and initially looks through the family and child files to ensure they are current and in compliance with all agency and CCL regulations. At some point and time, depending on the age of the child or children involved, the CCL representative will interview the child one-on-one, usually meeting him or her at school. Other children living in the home, whether foster children or birth children, will also be interviewed at some point to verify information. Foster parents are occasionally interviewed, but not always. CCL will come to the foster home at some point and complete a walkthrough. This is why we tell our foster parents to always have their home in compliance because you honestly never know when someone will come to the home and inspect it. Do not ever refuse to let a CCL representative in to the home. Do your best to be neutral and relaxed, even if the CCL representative speaks to you in cold, curt tones. This occurs more than you think. They are there to do their job and must be impartial all the way. They are not there to be your friend and give you accolades for being this giving person to foster children.

At some point after the interviews, home visits, and investigation, CCL returns to the agency to give their final findings on the case. The agency is informed of the findings who then can inform the foster parents of the findings. There are three types of possible end results: Substantiated, Unsubstantiated, and Inconclusive. Some agencies also use Unfounded. Obviously, Substantiated is the one you do not want. This means that in some way, shape, or form, the complaint in whole or parts was deemed true. Unsubstantiated is the most preferable of the three as it deems the complaint for all intensive purposes, as false. An Inconclusive complaint means the complaint can neither be identified as absolutely true or absolutely false. There may be some evidence to believe there may be some truth to the complaint.

In the agency I have worked for, whenever a complaint has been deemed Substantiated, and occasionally a few that have been deemed Inconclusive, the agency is required to come up with and complete a Plan of Correction. What this Plan will entail will depend on the Team that usually will include a supervisor, the CCL representative, and possibly the agency social worker on the case. Some Plan of Correction action items in the past have included specialized training on the issue at hand, getting whatever was not in compliance completed (such as if an updated Emergency Plan needs to be completed and posted), meeting with the agency social worker and/or supervisor to discuss the Complaint findings in detail and making an agreement on how to improve this situation should it happen again, and occasionally draw up a contract on how or what will occur next time a similar situation occurs.

I do not want to scare anyone off, but something to keep in mind is that too many Substantiated complaints can actually affect foster parents in the long term. These Substantiated complaints stack up and are put on the foster parents' criminal history record. At one point during my time here with the agency, a CCL representative actually informed our staff that if a foster parent had more than one complaint, regardless of the findings, within a 12-month timeframe the individual could not participate in any activity that required fingerprinting background checks, such as coaching or employment with children. Scary stuff!

All in all, being a foster parent is truly a difficult decision to make. It requires patience, understanding, adaptability, and commitment. It should be known that these rules were put in to place for a reason. These rules and regulations are here to protect children that have already been trumped with a traumatic beginning in life. True, at times some of the rules are frustrating and ridiculous, but they are here for the child's well being.

9

Foster/Adopt Parents

Foster and adoptive parents come in all shapes and sizes, and I mean that personality and history-wise. Unlike county social workers and agency social workers, foster and adoptive parents come with so many complex and different angles. With social workers, you can expect some similarities amongst them, but with foster parents, this is less the case.

Why a foster or adoptive parent comes to this process can be an indicator of what type of parent they will become for the children. Culture and personal upbringing can also play a factor. I will discuss a few examples of the types of foster parents I have either worked directly with or have heard stories (occasionally horror stories) from other social workers. As an agency, we do the best we can to weed out those individuals and couples who are doing this for all the wrong reasons ("only in it for the money" is one of the most common examples), but we can only get behind the facades so well. People know how to put on their best presentations in front of interviewers. Another factor I will discuss will also be long term effects that can occur.

The Good Ones

Every agency has a handful of phenomenal foster parents that make the agency's job a piece of cake. With our agency, several of these families came through to "give back to children in need" who came to us either as veterans from another foster agency or as "green" foster or adoptive parents. A "green" foster parent means very new to the process, and/or child rearing altogether. Good things about the veterans are they know what's expected of them, know how to handle situations of crisis with ease, request assistance from the agency when they know it is needed, and work well with professionals. A good thing about a "green" foster or adoptive family is they come in with a blank slate that can be molded.

A family that had been with the agency for over 17 years would be one that I would qualify as the veteran class. I have not worked directly with this family myself, but what they have done over the years is what I can only say is above and beyond the call of duty. The family began fostering as a couple, but the wife passed away in 2014 unexpectedly. Together they fostered or provided respite care for over 30 children (and that's just based on records since 2002). Most of the children the couple worked with were usually 10 and older, but there were the occasional young ones that stayed a short time. The family has done phenomenal work with older children and youth, maintained connections with several of them after reunifying with birth family or emancipating out of the system. The couple worked with a handful or more of ITFC foster youth who demonstrated a higher need of services and supports. The couple always worked well with agency staff, county staff, birth families, and other people involved in the children's cases. Even as a single parent today, the husband continues to be a pride for the agency as he continues to be a support for three youth who had been in the home since before the passing of his wife.

My "green" family is one that I worked with for two years as a foster care social worker, and on and off during another year as the adoption social worker. Although this couple came to our agency as generally experienced foster parents, they were "green" in a few areas and blossomed. While living out of state, the couple were foster parents through the Department of Social Services (DSS) and provided care mainly for a couple of children with developmental delays. After moving to California due to a natural disaster, the family became certified with our agency. With the assistance of a longtime experienced agency social worker, the couple went from specializing in children with physical and developmental delays to working with and providing care for children who qualified for ITFC services as well. The couple has worked with some very difficult children over the last nine or so years, and even adopted a special needs young man in 2014. In this context, I mean special needs as most people would believe special needs as meaning. The child was a regional center client and had the following issues: seizure disorder, mild mental retardation, and Autism diagnosis. At the time of this writing, the couple continues to care for a child receiving ITFC services for behavioral issues as well as a severely developmentally delayed adolescent who qualified for ITFC services for his special needs. The adolescent is also a regional center client. The couple has provided care for over 30 children as long term placements, short term placements, or respites.

I also want to add a single parent of "honorable mention." This woman has been instrumental in the caring for a child with severe behavioral problems. If the child could not remain with the current foster mother, he would definitely find his way in to a group home or treatment facility of some kind because of his extreme behaviors. The child, who is eight years old, has been diagnosed as Attention Deficit/Hyperactivity Disorder(ADHD) and Oppositional Defiant Disorder (ODD). The child has temper tantrums, meltdowns, and can be physically aggressive with others. This foster parent has also been a phenomenal go-to foster parent for emergency placements, emergency respites, and taking difficult children and youth, most of which qualify for ITFC services. She has provided care for over 50 children since 2000.

The Quirky Ones

There are those foster parents that some agency social workers or other staff will have this look on their face when the foster parent or foster parents are approaching or being discussed that says, "Oh my Lord!" Actually, staff from other agencies may have the same response. These foster parents are quirky and unique either by the way they speak, what they say, how they look, or how they interact with others. I often get linked with these types of foster parents, but I cannot complain since I am a bit quirky myself. Sometimes, this uniqueness just fits together, not just with the agency social worker, but with the foster children as well.

There was a foster mother I worked with during my first two years as a social worker. She was unusual in so many ways, but we got a long well together. The foster mother was married, but the foster father was often away for long stretches of time due to the nature of his work. That does not mean I never met him. I enjoyed working with him as well, when I did have a chance to interact with him, and I know he had an influence on the boys that lived in the home at any given time. However, since the foster father was gone the majority of the time, I interacted mainly with the foster mother. She was one of those types who would call me regularly during the week. The foster mother worked with ITFC children so weekly visits were mandatory. Yet she managed to call me almost daily whether to check in, report something, vent, or simply chat. The foster mother was well known around the office that if she caught you in a conversation, whether by phone or in the office, she would have your attention for a minimum of 20 minutes. There were a minimum of two children placed in her home at any given time. She enjoyed being busy, having children and youth around, and simply being involved. From 2005 to 2010, the couple cared for up to 35 children. One of those was adopted at 17 years old who was a developmentally delayed, regional center client. It was a spectacular experience, to transfer from the foster care social worker to the adoption social worker within a month or less of the adoption. I was able to follow this one to the end. It was a wonderful feeling! This foster family was notorious for taking in very difficult children and youth. In fact, this couple ended up taking in, though briefly, some of our more difficult children and youth during a period of time. Unfortunately, several of them ended up leaving the home, needing a higher level of care. It was a family I was grateful to have as a part of my beginning experience as a social worker.

At the time of this writing, I have been working with a single foster parent who others in the office find unusual and quirky. However, with the two children she came to the agency in her placement, a person would have to be different and open to uniqueness. The foster mother has been with the agency for over two years. She came to our agency from a couple of other agencies that would end up closing their doors (is that a bad omen?). At the time of her certification with our agency, the foster mother had twin girls living in her home. The girls had been living with her for a little over a year by the time I began to work with them. To say these twin girls were a handful is putting it mildly. Within two years, both girls would be on their way to separate group homes because of the severity of their behaviors. This was crushing for the foster mother who looked on these girls as her family, and still does to this day. She will have open doors to both girls should they ever decide to come back knocking. The foster mother is currently caring for another difficult young lady. The twins who previously lived in the home had received ITFC services, one of them received TBS services, both received mental health services, and still they could not maintain their behaviors in the home, school, or community. The youth currently in the home struggles with allowing herself to become part of a family without conflict. Although the foster mother has been frustrated and overwhelmed with the children she has cared for over the past two or more years, she always has a sense of humor, almost a crazy type of sense of humor. But this works under the circumstances. You almost need a crazy type of sense of humor at times to do this kind of work. I enjoy working with the foster mother as she keeps me on my toes and still manages to keep humor alive even when most people would think you cannot.

The Bad Ones

Okay, so there are those foster parents out there who are looking for a quick buck. The amusing part is, I do not think those who come through to become foster parents realize it is not really an easy way to make a quick buck. I often say, for a 24 hour job, the pay really is not that good if you think about it. But, truthfully, there will be those types who make it through who are only in it for the money. And then there are those that are just generally not good parenting material in general.

One of the more horrific foster parent stories I have heard from our agency was from several years ago. I was not working with this family, thank goodness, or I may have had a nervous breakdown. We teach our foster parents that religion is not pushed on our foster children. If you do, this is a personal rights violation. In fact, if the children choose to attend another form of religious services than practiced by the foster parents, measures are taken to assure the children can practice whatever faith they practice. There was a single foster parent who began taking care of one our longtime youth. She was a fairly new foster parent. The agency soon found out that the foster parent tried to exorcize demons from our foster youth. Say what?! The youth was in the foster home for barely two months, was baptized, had her clothing taken from her and was instructed to dress and wear her hair a specific way. Needless to say, the foster parent was certified with our agency for less than one year.

When I first began working with the agency, I was made aware of a couple that was then certified with us. I never directly worked with the couple, but they were one of those that you did not want to be seen out in public. During a foster parent appreciation picnic event, the woman came to the event dressed inappropriately. First of all, there are young men present. Second of all, many of these children have issues around boundaries, both in general and sexually. The couple was often seen taking little things as if they were poor, and it was in excess. If there were left over food items at an event, they would do their best to grab as much, without consideration to others, as possible. There were also concerns about supervision, cleanliness (both the home and their persons), and discipline. The couple stayed certified longer than I would have wanted, but that was mainly due to the last two placements in the home were extended family members. Staff always went in the opposite direction when this family came around.

As a person writing homestudies for foster and adoptive parents coming through the process, it is my duty to determine if a couple or single parent are appropriate, ready, and able to do the duties at hand. There are the moments when I have that gut feeling something is not quite right, but without something concrete to grasp at, I have to proceed. There were two scenarios like this that I had experienced. One that, thankfully, went away on its own, and the other that became a problem.

In the first scenario, after interviewing the couple, I had this nagging feeling that something was not quite right. Numbers did not add up, financially. I told the family in order to complete their homestudy, I would need proof of the "child support" income that was included on their budget form. This may seem silly to the reader, but without proof of this stated income, the finances did not add up. After a couple of months with no response, we were able to discontinue with the family. The child support was a couple of hundred dollars, but based on the budget form the couple completed, without that support, they could not financially support themselves. Then I also had to factor in that the daughter who was the purpose of the claimed "child support" would be turning 18 in a couple of months, concluding this "income" would no longer be there for support. So, where would the extra two hundred dollars come from just to support this family on a regular basis? I had a feeling the family was coming through solely for the money.

The second scenario was much more gray, than black and white. There were things that did not come together, but I could not put my finger on it.

I did my best to stall the process where I could, hoping the family would give up and move on to another agency. I had a feeling this family, too, was coming through for the money. But I did not have anything that I could use to delay the process further, though now I wish I had. There was one placement that pretty much was the end of it all. Although this was a very difficult child who had been placed in a few homes over the last couple of years, it would be a dramatic end for the child, the agency, and for me personally. Everything was reportedly going well, based on reports by the agency social worker. The foster family was planning to adopt the child. This sounded fantastic, as the child was well known among staff. However, before the adoption plan could proceed, an external complaint came in that the foster parents were excessively disciplining the child, and not only at home but in the community as well. And the complaint and concerns came from two separate sources. The sources themselves ended up being mind-blowing as well, a church member and a family member of the foster parents. The child was moved yet again and shortly there after the family was decertified from our agency. That one left a bad taste in my mouth!

End Game

There is another wrong reason to become a foster parent or adoptive parent. When one parent is 100% on board to become a foster or adoptive parent, and the other parent is "only doing this to support my" spouse, that is a very wrong reason. If a couple comes in to this thinking this will bring them together, this is most likely not the case. This is not to say that some relationships do not grow stronger with a child involved, but if the relationship is weak before a child comes in to the fold, this is a disaster waiting to happen. I do not wish to scare people off from becoming foster or adoptive parents, but this must be a mutual decision. Over the past nine years, about a half a dozen or so couples have separated or divorced, whether after providing care together, or before a child has ever been placed in the home. Being a foster parent is not an easy task. If you go in as a team, you need to work together as a team to the end. The decision to becoming a foster or adoptive parent is not just about you. It's also about these children that need stability, not more chaos and disruption.

10

Foster Children and Youth

As part of a treatment foster care agency, I have seen many different types of children come in and out of the system. Children can be anywhere from a few weeks old up to 20 years old. The children and youth that the agency I work for serves are usually considered "the hard to place" children. These children are hard to place based on any number of factors. Treatment foster care is sought for large sibling sets, sibling sets that have older children as well as younger children, children with difficult behaviors, special needs children, or a population that most foster parents prefer not to work with such as adolescents. Most foster parents come through wanting that one perfect little baby. That is not our agency's reality. If we get a placement call for an infant, it is usually a drug-exposed infant or premature infant. Our agency has had the occasional luck of getting the "perfect baby" placed, but the baby usually reunifies with the birth family or moves with extended family members. The truth of the matter is, children and youth come in to the system of all ages, with unpredictable baggage and trauma, which need just as much love and security as that perfect little baby.

The Honeymoon

Whenever children first move to a home, they tend to behave like perfect little angels. That's not to say that some children who come in to foster care are not capable of being perfect little angels long term, but what is typical of a child's "normal" behavior does not show up until after the honeymoon. The honeymoon period is an unspecified time frame where a child who comes in to foster care acts on their best behavior. This behavior and honeymoon period can last anywhere from a couple of hours to several months.

What I tell foster parents is to be prepared for the "perfect little angel" to begin acting different and extreme at any given time without warning. Although most foster parents wish the child would remain in the honeymoon period forever, that is not realistic. A positive thing about the honeymoon period ending is the truth that the child has become comfortable and feels safe enough to act like who he or she really is. The point of a good foster home is be that safe haven for a child to respond to his or her situation in a safe place where the child can learn how to cope with the situations he or she was removed from. Enjoy the honeymoon period, but expect that there will be an end so you are prepared.

Recipe for Success

I have heard a few times from adults that all foster children and youth need is love. Love is all they need. Though it is true that foster children do need love, (who doesn't?), they need much more than that. Some of these children need unconditional love. A child should never be expected to feel grateful that you, a stranger, took him or her in to your care. Why should a child be grateful that other people decided that her parents were not doing their job as a parent correctly? Although, yes, foster children do need love, they need more than just love.

One of the bigger issues that always is brought up with foster children, whether from professionals or from the foster children themselves, is trust is a big word. Trust is more paramount than love. Foster children come in to the system after experiencing a situation where they do not know if or when they can trust their own parents. Strangers, such as law enforcement and CPS, come in and take children away from their parents, the only people foster children had any relevant trust in to begin with. The foster children are then thrust in to a strange new home, with strange new people, with strange new rules. In the drop of a hat, these new strangers can make the foster children leave for no apparent reason. Just when a child begins to trust an adult, something usually occurs to make the child question that trust, whether the adult directly caused for the reason of mistrust or this "system" the child was thrown in to unwillingly. It is quite the uphill battle to try to earn a foster child's trust. Even when you think you may have earned it, you are tested or proven wrong.

Foster children and youth need unconditional love, unconditional trust, and unconditional commitment. I think as a world, we need to realize these children are going to be taking care of us someday. We should give them what they need now so they are ready for the world and the future when it is their time.

The Labels

When a foster parent becomes certified through our agency, one of the key teaching lessons is reminding him or her never to identify the foster child as such. When introducing a foster child to outsiders, or even to extended family, avoid identifying the child as "this is my foster son (or daughter)." Foster children and youth have quite a bit to live up to even without the label of being a "foster child" and putting that label on them makes their life more difficult.

Not all foster children fall in to the typical foster child myth. When people think of foster children they think "poor," "un-kept," "behavior problems," "dropout," "runaway," "bad kids," and other negative things, but this is not altogether true. Yes there are some children from the foster system that fall in to these myths, unwillingly, but there are children and youth that are just like every other child. Smart, well mannered, follows rules, respectful, engaging, and so many other positive aspects.

Unfortunately though, the majority of the population who do not know the details and specifics behind foster care believe the myths on face value. This becomes even more complicated when public entities, like the schools and law enforcement, immediately assume the myths are true for all foster children and youth. I try to teach some of our foster children not to identify themselves as foster children, although some do. This will often bring with it problems of others treating them like the foster care myths are true.

I have observed teachers and schools more or less give up on foster children, or even the reverse, and continue to "try" when the original plan continues to fail the child. There are policies in place, such as in the schools, in an effort to assist foster children in progressing and succeeding in school as this is often an area of struggle. However, some of these policies tend to interrupt progress and success, and continue to allow foster children to be stuck and continue to fail. As with most policies and rules, this is an area that can continue to use some work.

People do not like being labeled in general. Foster children are no different.

One Diagnosis, Two Diagnoses, Three Diagnoses

Another concern in foster care is labeling children based on a diagnosis. It is more common to see children in foster care diagnosed with a mental health disorder compared to children not in the system. There continues to be an argument that there are way too many children, in foster care and in general, being diagnosed with Attention Deficit/Hyperactivity Disorder (ADHD). I agree with this argument. The problem with children diagnosed with ADHD is the fact that some of these children come from an unstructured environment and are then forced in to a structured environment and expected to sit still and produce. This is not a very realistic expectation.

There are a handful of disorders that foster children and youth are commonly diagnosed with such ADHD, depression, anxiety disorders, Post Traumatic Stress Disorder (PTSD), Reactive Attachment Disorder (RAD), Oppositional Defiant Disorder (ODD), and Bipolar Disorder. These are not the exclusive disorders diagnosed in foster care, but are generally the most common.

PTSD has only recently been attached to children in foster care. Although most people think of soldiers and war veterans, rape survivors,

survivors of natural disasters, and survivors of assaults or horrific accidents when this disorder is mentioned, this disorder encompasses any person who has experienced a traumatic event or situation that is re-lived over and over again after the event has occurred. I know of a child who would always sit facing exits, ensuring there was one close by at all times. When you have been put in a traumatic situation where there appears to be no exit, a person can become hyper vigilant and overly aware to this in future situations, whether traumatic or not.

Another diagnosis that appears to be picking up steam lately is Reactive Attachment Disorder (RAD). I honestly was skeptical of this disorder until I actually began working with children who demonstrated this disorder to the perfection. This is actually a very difficult disorder to deal with and requires above and beyond amounts of patience, unconditional love, and commitment. Many of the children diagnosed with this disorder, or who demonstrate signs of this disorder, commonly end up bouncing from home to home, or in a group home or residential treatment facility. These children, due to their traumas and experiences, cannot, or will not, attach to others.

Although a diagnosis is necessary in some instances, especially if this helps determine a means of support and services that can treat the disorder, a child should not be identified based on a diagnosis. A diagnosis can follow people throughout their life, and not always in a positive manner. A child, and person, is more than a diagnosis.

Psychotropic Medication

The war is on regarding the excess in over medicating children in the system. Well, over medicating children in general is a nationwide problem, but the children in the foster care system do not have the means of advocacy for them against over prescribing psychotropic medication. When a child is acting out, the first thing that is done is a diagnosis is given. Second on the list, prescribing psychotropic medication. The problem with many psychotropic medications is the fact that honest testing was never completed on how psychotropic medications affected children and adolescents. Most testing is completed and approved on adults, not children and adolescents.

The fact about psychotropic medication that people tend to ignore is that the medication is supposed to be a short term solution. Medication is prescribed to curve the immediately problem, such as lower the anxiety level so an individual can leave their home. The long term solution is getting the individual in to therapy, utilizing psychotropic medication along with therapy to treat the problem. Eventually the goal is to reduce the psychotropic medication and decrease the need of therapy. Unfortunately, many people see psychotropic medication as a quick fix-it solution, which only really shadows the overlying problem.

It is true that there are circumstances where prescribing medication is necessary, for safety purposes or for legitimate diagnoses that require long term medication therapy such as a legitimate diagnosis of bipolar disorder. But this practice needs to be monitored more closely, as there are young children and youth out there taking a couple to several very strong acting psychotropic medications at a time. It can be pretty scary!

As the foster or adoptive parents, or even as the social worker, our job is to advocate for a population that often cannot advocate for themselves.

11

Birth Families

Of course, I cannot discuss foster care without discussing the birth families. Without birth families struggling, there would be no foster care system. Unfortunately, birth families get a bad rep before the process even begins. There are those true horror stories of birth families who do not or will not change their ways, even for their children, or treat their children as inferior beings. But there are also those birth families who are truly just struggling and needed the help and support to get the family back on the right path. Another factor to all this is the truly strong need to protect these children by the foster parents, social workers, and other professionals involved, whether we know what is truly good for them or not. I often teach my foster families to remain neutral in the presence of the birth families, try to make some connection however superficial, and never speak negatively of the birth family in the child's presence. These factors can influence how successful or unsuccessful a placement will be as well as the birth families progress.

The Lost Causes

Unfortunately there are those stories where the birth parents or birth families live up to all of those horrible rumors and myths that are commonly associated with people who have their children in the system. A parent who loses his or her children who as some people say, "should never have had children." And it's true, there are people who should never have had children. Not all people were made to be parents and role models.

There are those birth family members who step in and do what they are being told to do by child welfare, but often times it is not for the right reasons. Some family members get pressured in to stepping up on behalf of their adult child, their nephew, their niece, their grandchildren, because its family. The stigma is that family should not be in the system. However, some family members are not prepared to care for other people's children, for any number of reasons.

There are those parents that have either lost other children to the system at another time and know how to "work" the system, or simply do not bother to do anything to get their children back. Some parents leave the county, leave the state, to avoid further repercussions for their poor attempts at parenting. Lose their children and can get a "get out of jail" free card and continue on with their lives without batting an eyelash.

There are those birth parents who are given the benefit of the doubt, even when they should not, by having visits increased, a plan to reunify still a go, or children returning in a fairly quick amount of time yet the birth parents did some awful things to lose their children in the first place. It is a very scary place to be for a foster parent and social worker. The purpose is to believe and hope for second chances even in times when the worst is expected.

There are birth parents who will buck the system in attempt to make themselves look better, attempt to make every one else from "the system" as the bad guys, all the while not taking accountability for their own actions. The seasoned parent, who is all very well aware of the systems rules, would know if he or she misses three visits in a row, visits will be canceled. So the parent misses two and shows for the third. This is in no way fair to the children, but the system allows this.

These are the parents and birth families that make this business difficult. And unfortunately, yes, foster care is looked on as a form of business. Agencies advertise for foster parent to join their agencies through employment classifieds in local newspapers. Foster parents are in an underpaid job however. But, I digress.

I have foster parents who end up venting to me about why scheduled visits remain necessary, especially in long term foster care, when the birth parent does not always regularly make it for these visits. The reason is, the children obviously still need these connections. Imagine moving in with a stranger and losing every single one of your family members. The loss is not by death, the family is still out there in the world, but you never get to see them or talk to them, and not by choice. It is just what it is. Not a pleasant thought, is it?

There is not much that can be done with these types of birth families other than absolute patience, tolerance, and hope on the part of the foster parent and social workers. Its all a waiting game.

The Fighters

There are those birth families who honestly become a part of the system simply due to hard times and bad luck. The truth is we all make mistakes, but there are those people who can either get away with them with little repercussions or learn from them quickly. And then there are those who slip and their children pay the consequences.

I have worked with foster families who were above and beyond supportive in the birth families progress, leading to reunification and a healthier situation for the child or children in the long run. There are even foster parents who continue to be a support to birth families, years later, and continue to be there to encourage and support a birth family through any sudden struggles.

There are those situations where a parent needed the wake up call that the decisions and choices he or she was making was not in the best interest of his or her child or children, or even in their own best interest. There truly have been birth families who wanted their children back with the family and made active efforts to get this done.

The hardest part is working with children in foster care without truly having an understanding of where the birth parents are coming from. Substance abuse and domestic violence are the more common reasons behind children entering the system. If you have never had experience with either of these issues, you are not going to know what the birth parent is up against. Realistically, any person is capable of falling prey to either of these obstacles, and they are very real obstacles to overcome.

When a birth parent is successful at reunifying with his or her child or children, it really is a remarkable success. Especially in those circumstances where the birth parent did everything possible, minus a few hiccups on the way, and made it to the other side. Truly remarkable!

Unfortunately, all birth families get the short end of the stick immediately. The initial response of those of us on the other side is to blame the birth family without consideration of their situation or circumstances. There are plenty of people and families out there in the world that we see doing wrong, or doing inappropriate or odd things, and we automatically think, "they should have their children taken away from them. They don't know how to be parents." Truthfully, we do not take classes or have mentors teaching us how to be a parent. We have to learn as we go. Some parents are not given opportunities to learn from previous parenting figures or role models and are doing the best they can with what they have. Yes there are parents out there that truly should not have been or should ever be parents, but there are also those parents who simply need a helping hand with encouragement, support, and skills. Everyone deserves a second chance and an opportunity to explain their actions, and birth parents are no different.

12

A Few Experiences for the Road

I could tell many different stories of the experiences I have had over the years with foster children and youth, and I will likely write another book simply about the many different children our agency has served over the years, but for now, I chose to pick five stories to share. Two stories are tragic, two stories are wonderful successes, and one story is neither a tragedy nor a success. These stories have left profound impressions on me for different reasons.

The First Adoption Success

I mentioned this scenario earlier in the Foster and Adoptive Parent chapter, but this case was a success for several reasons and worthy of sharing again. I was the foster care social worker for this young man for two years. He was one of two children who were permanent fixtures in the foster home during my two years as a foster care social worker. The other child would eventually leave the home once I became an adoption social worker, but that is another story. I began working with this young man when he was 15 years old. I will call him David. For obvious confidentiality reasons, I will not use his or other children's real names.

David was a regional center client because he had the mentality of an eight or nine year old in a 15 year old's body. David was a sweetheart, and could never do wrong. He had areas that required learning new skills on an ongoing basis such as how to interact appropriately with peers, especially peers of the opposite sex. Amusingly, David would be picked on by others due to his developmental delays yet there were just as many peers and adults that stood up for and were protective of him on a regular basis. David's is one of those rare cases because he was adopted with his special needs and all, at the age of 17 years old.

People tend not to think about adopting older children, even though I have witnessed older adolescents being adopted. What made this case more special was the fact I carried the case for two years as a foster care social worker. Just as I was in the process of transferring to an adoption social worker position, David was adopted. I was the foster care social worker and the adoption social worker. I was able to be there through the end. It was an amazing case, and one that ended the way you always hope one does, with love, security, and hope.

The Failed Adoption

He was a three year old little boy who lost his forever family in the blink of an eye. The worst part is, none of us at the agency saw it coming. The little boy was nicknamed Peanut by the foster father. Peanut was little for his age. I picked him up on a few occasions as he like to be held, and he was light as a feather. He was a cute, but hyper little boy. As in the previous case I shared, I began as the foster care social worker for this child and family, and continued with the family after I transferred to adoptions. That's when the case became a nightmare.

I was updating the family's homestudy for the adoption of Peanut. We were literally a few pieces of information away from completing the homestudy, when I was informed the family no longer wanted to proceed with the adoption. I was in shock! I felt like someone had hit me with a truck. I knew Peanut could be a handful at times, a bit too hyper, occasionally physically aggressive in daycare, but nothing that made me think the family would change their mind about adopting him. Although as an adoption social worker I usually have less contact with a family then a foster care social worker would, I continued to stay heavily involved in the case to the end. After meetings and discussions with the family, agency social worker, and county social worker, separately, it was discovered that the foster mother and one foster daughter apparently did not feel a connection to Peanut. The foster father and older foster daughter, on the other hand, were strongly attached.

The part that angered me the most was why this family waited until the adoption was on the horizon. They just allowed this little boy to spend all of this time attaching to them (a year and a half), just so they could hand him back and say half of the family was not, in turn, attached to Peanut. I became overly helpful to the county social worker while she found another potential adoptive home for Peanut because I felt responsible and guilty for not knowing the truth sooner. The foster father and older foster daughter were obviously devastated by the move while the foster mother and younger foster daughter barely blinked. A few months after the move, I occasionally would get calls from the foster father, who was no longer certified with the agency for obvious reasons, checking in to see if I had heard anything about Peanut. The last either of us heard was that the new adoptive home was not going well. I often wonder where little Peanut is, and I hope with all my heart he finally found his forever home.

The Lost One

This story is not really either a success story or a tragedy. This story just is. When I first began working for the agency, a wet-behind-the-ears foster care social worker, I was given the case of a 10 year old female. I will call her Kara. Kara was a difficult child for the least expected reason. She would shut down and not speak, which can be more frustrating than those children that have outbursts and tantrums. She was also a bully and did some unusual things to her "friends." She would show up at their houses, occasionally getting them in to trouble, trip them, push them, say mean things, and do things that a real friend would not do. She was defiant in school and at home, though her defiance often was demonstrated in silence.

I was Kara's social worker for two years. During that time, Kara did some pretty scary and disturbing things for a 10 to 12 year old. The supervision was not what it should have been as the single foster mother was a working individual. However, Kara used this to her advantage. On a few occasions during the first year and a half, Kara would not be where she was supposed to be, whether at the after school program or the daycare. On one of these occasions, she did not return home from wherever she was until 9 p.m. at night. On another occasion, Kara went to a friend's home without permission, who was not supposed to be interacting with Kara, who ended up getting grounded. The worst part was, when the foster mother and I were discussing this situation with her, she had a smirk on her face.

The unfortunate truth about Kara is she really had the history and experience that you wish no one should ever have. Kara was removed from her birth family because at least Kara was sexually abused by the father, among other things. Kara was placed with two older brothers and a younger brother for awhile, but the two older brother became too much to handle. The two older brothers would each end up spending time in group homes. Kara lived in a potential adoptive home with her youngest brother. However, something happened that resulted in Kara being moved while her brother remained and was adopted. Kara never really could understand or accepted this. Not that she should have.

Although I was no longer her social worker because I transferred to adoptions, I kept my ear open whenever her name came up. She continued to struggle throughout the years. She moved from home to home. I honestly believe that Kara struggled with attachments overall. She would say she wants to be adopted, already had a name she wanted to change her name to, and was overly excited when she spoke about some day being adopted. Kara remained in foster care through our agency from age 10 years old to 18 years old when she emancipated out of the system. During that time, Kara had seven placements. The shortest placement lasted months, the longest lasted almost three years.

I struggled with Kara's case during and after working with her. She was a stubborn and difficult child, but I always wanted what was best for her. There are those people who come through your life you just gravitate towards and naturally care about. Kara was one of those people for me. I hope she is able to work through her past at some point, and have a productive and happy future.

A Beginner's Tragedy

I had been a social worker for approximately six months when I was dealt my first tragedy. Jake, 12, was a difficult youth as he often argued with both adults and peers. He did not accept consequences for his actions well, and would often require more consequences on top of his original consequences. Jake could be outgoing and personable, but often complained about others, complained about school, complained about things in general, and he rarely accepted accountability for his actions.

Jake had been placed with his first foster family for a little over four years. The family was a veteran family who had been with the agency for approximately 14 years by this point. They could no longer care for him as he became too disruptive and would not follow rules. This continued in the home he was placed in when I began working at the agency. However, there appeared not to be a honeymoon period. He clashed with everyone in the house, which kept the home in an uproar and on edge pretty much until he was moved from the home. When his last placement gave a 30 day notice on him after living in the home for approximately six months or so, it was a shock when the county social worker immediately decided, without telling the youth, that his next placement would be a group home.

First of all, I have my own personal opinion of group homes that is in no way a positive one. This opinion is based solely on experience I had working in group homes with clients who were receiving TBS services, or working with clients with TBS services that attended nonpublic schools. Children and youth who have behavioral problems determined not to be fit for mainstream classes or even special education classes are often referred to nonpublic schools. Several children and youth who attend nonpublic schools are living in group homes, though others live in foster homes or with the birth family.

Second, I found the youth annoying at times, but did not feel he was suitable for a group home. Of course, I was a new social worker and may have been wrong in my opinion, but it was what it was. I was too new to feel I could disagree with the county worker. And unfortunately our agency did not have a back up option of a home either.

Even though the foster mother was beyond frustrated with the youth and the chaos he caused in her home, the foster mother had done well with staying in contact with an older sister who had previously emancipated out of foster care herself. Jake had a difficult upbringing. Jake was one of several siblings that were removed from the birth family's care. Jake was the youngest. The one thing that appeared to reach Jake while I was working with him was his connection with his sister and family. The sister was the only one who made an active effort to call, check in, or visit Jake on a regular basis. Other relatives, such as brothers, the father, or grandparent, would keep in contact irregularly. The only thing that appeared to keep Jake on track in any way was his sister.

The day Jake was taken to the group home was the day he found out he was going to a group home. I have always disliked this practice. These kids struggle with enough uncertainty and unpredictable situations. After Jake was moved to the group home, the county worker said that visits with family are usually put on hold for up to two months while the child stabilizes. I did not like the sound of that. Jake relied on his visits.

I found out through a co-worker who worked with the first family Jake lived with that Jake had died. It was a little over one month after leaving the agency, and only a couple of weeks after Jake turned 13 years old. It was devastating news. The truth behind his death is unknown. What I was told was he was found hanging by a belt. Unfortunately, the assumption is he either committed suicide or he was doing the "strangling game." It was big around this time that older children and youth were dying from choking themselves for the high or sexual gratification. I will never know. But it was a devastating blow. I was questioning my abilities as a social worker for months until fellow co-workers reminded me Jake was the one responsible, and he never spoke of such things. There were no signs to suspect suicide. The case haunts me to this day. Something like that you never forget.

A Forever Family

This foster mother made no bones that she did not like "the system" and would push against the grain whenever she could. However, she was driven for what was in the best interest of her girls. The foster mother had adopted two sisters, at different timelines in the process, when she took in three sisters. It was one of those very rare cases that could be truly identified as low risk. The girls were moved from an adoptive home where the adoptive "mother" was an older woman of a different ethnic background. The adoptive mother had a stroke, and it was highly likely from the get-go the girls would be available for adoption with little obstacles. Even as a low risk placement, the timeline from placement to adoption finalization was one year and four months.

The two older girls who had been adopted previously would be considered the ones with behavioral issues compared to these three girls. Although there were minor issues over the year, the issues were based more on strong personality differences than behavioral concerns normally associated with children in foster care.

Sara was the oldest of the three and was the pleaser. Sara almost always presented as the "good girl", always had a smile on her face and had little to say. Anna was the middle sister, and acted as such. She was very dramatic, and appeared sad or mad at the beginning of most visits I had with her. Anna was the most challenging of the three because of her dramatic nature. However, she apparently had the strongest talent for singing of her three sisters. Katy was the baby and often took advantage of this. She was often doted on by the older adopted sisters. Amusingly Katy struggled with enuresis (wetting herself) about one to two months in to her placement. It was the kind of issue the county did not know about, and was an issue with the foster mother. Thankfully, after the foster mother had to leave work for several weeks due to health issues, the enuresis decreased considerably until it was no longer a concern.

An interesting piece of the story is that the foster mother had a really strong work ethic, so strong it drove her most of her adult life. When the three youngest girls moved to the home, this drive changed from her focus on work to her focus on her family. The foster mother was one of those types you want the children to have, frequently taking the family on weekend getaways, traveling out of state for church events, and a generally very active foster parent. Each girl was involved in an activity outside of school that encouraged their individual talents (one was in an art class, one was involved in singing classes, and two of them were involved in piano lessons).

At times the foster mother was very frustrating to work with from a social worker's standpoint, but the ultimate goal for her was to do what was best for each of her girls, and build her forever family. I loved attending the finalizations for all five girls. I was the adoption social worker only for the two oldest girls, but attended their adoption finalizations. I was the foster care and adoption social worker for the younger three girls. The adoption finalizations in the courtroom with the family were spectacular events. Each of the girls were dressed in the most beautiful dresses, their hair done up, new shoes on, and looking their best. I loved being apart of their beginning, and I loved this kind of ending. Watching the foster mother cry as she was signing the finalization paperwork was a heart warming feeling. It is because of the cases like this one that I am able to get rejuvenated in a job that can otherwise be overwhelming and heart breaking at times. A forever family was made!

13

A Degree Above All Others

As a disclaimer to the reader, this chapter is more of a vent on my part. If I become too annoying, negative, or off topic for you, feel free to skip this chapter. However, I feel this needs to be discussed.

As I mentioned in the introduction, there was a time when one of the social work associations began to argue that any person with a degree other than in social work was deemed not worthy or professional enough for someone in a social worker position. I know of a few social workers who have degrees in psychology, counseling, child development, and others that have done a phenomenal job as a social worker. To discount the work that many of these individuals have done over the years is a disservice.

As a social worker with a masters in counseling, I cannot directly identify in other professionals if their masters is in counseling, psychology, social worker, or something entirely different. The same can be said for foster parents. Most foster parents could not tell the difference between a social worker with a degree in social work versus a social worker with a degree in another field. As long as the job is getting done, I'm not sure why the need for an argument.

For those of you who do not know, social work degrees can lead an individual to being licensed as Licensed Clinical Social Workers (LCSW). As an LCSW, the individual can provide therapy like a therapist would. If we are going to argue that an individual who is on the Marriage and Family Therapist (MFT) track should not be allowed to be a social worker because the degree is not in social work, than that opens up the argument to why should an LCSW be allowed to provide therapy if the person does not have a degree in therapy or counseling.

I have been a social worker for nine years. I admit I may not be the best social worker, maybe not even a great social worker, but I am a good social worker and I can get the job done. To say I am not deserving of this job because of my degree is a slap in the face. It truly takes a special kind of individual to be a social worker, just as it takes a special kind of individual to be a county social worker or foster parent.

Not all people who end up with a degree in counseling actually end up working in counseling or therapy directly. And not all individuals with degrees in social work end up being social workers, whether by choice or not. Social work is a complex, intense form of work. It is not easy in any way, shape, or form, and it requires an adaptability and quality that not all people have.

Epilogue

By 2019 most licensed foster care and adoption agencies will be required to have an adoptions license in California. An alternative to this is a foster care agency must have an approved agreement with an adoption agency who can complete the adoption requirements on the foster care agency's behalf in order for the foster care agency to continue to receive foster care placements. I have heard from a few local agencies that they are in the process of getting their adoption license. The one major downfall to this is the competition for finding foster parents and receiving foster care placements will increase considerably. This is another step away from long term foster care, and attempting to get the children out of the system as quickly as possible.

For agencies, this will become complicated and it will be every agency for them self. The agency I have worked for had two qualities that allowed us to stand out as a "premier" FFA: we have had our adoption license for a decade or more, and we provide the intensive treatment services. Once other agencies get their license, our agency will no longer be premier, and we will have to fight our way to stay in business.

For those who have always wanted to be just a *foster* parent with the only intent of caring for someone short term who would reunify or long term without adoption or guardianship, this change will be complicated. The big push will be the child or children reunify, or the only other alternative is permanency, preferably adoption or legal guardianship. This upcoming change will be interesting to see how it plays out in the long term.

I would like to take a moment to mention the recently published book, *Welcome to the Roller Coaster*, by D.D. Foster. For general purposes I would recommend this book for anyone who is considering becoming a foster parent or newly certified foster parents. It gives a taste of what a foster parent may experience. The book is a collection of experiences of more than a dozen foster mothers. There are pros and there are cons to the book, from an agency social worker's perspective.

The pros of the book are obvious. There are heart warming experiences and heart breaking experiences. This is typical of foster care and adoption. There are experiences of some of the different professionals involved in the process. There is a general explanation of the complexity of the foster care and adoption process. Special needs children are adoptable. Birth family contacts and connections can be positive. Being a foster parent is not easy.

The cons of the book are minor, but should be noted. I was disappointed that there were only stories by foster mothers, and none by foster fathers. Our agency has a handful of phenomenal single fathers, and phenomenal married foster fathers, that can give some of the stories in this book a run for their money. Most of the children were 10 years old or younger, with the exception of the teen mother. Some of the true stories I have memorable experiences of are the older children. There is little information if any of the stories were from foster care agencies or if they were primarily county foster homes. There is a significant difference between county foster parents and nonprofit foster care agency foster parents.

All in all, though, I think the book is a good read for foster parents and new social workers alike. I heard there is a second book in the works, which is fantastic. There is not enough information out there about foster care and adoption.

Although the foster care and adoption world can be frustrating, heart breaking, confusing, and stressful, I would not have traded the experiences I have had over the past nine years for anything. I once bragged I had my hand in 75 adoptions over the course of five years. That's just my adoption adventures. My foster care adventures are probably even more dramatic. I have met so many wonderful, different, and interesting people and children over the last nine years. No matter where I go from here, whether I stay in foster care and adoptions for the long haul, or change to another population to serve, this experience has shaped me in to the person I have become. It will always remain a part of me; the good, the bad, and the ugly.

Non-Related Extended Family Member (NREFM) information

http://advokids.org/legal-tools/information-for-relatives-2/

SFCASA.org

http://www.sfcasa.org/the-crisis/california-national-statistics/

Supporting THP+ for California's Emancipating Foster Youth: A Compilation of Statistics.

http://www.ballantinesbiz.com/everychild/emancipatingfosteryouthstatistics.htm

California Youth Connection

http://www.calyouthconn.org/ab12-implementation

John Burton Foundation on AB 12:

http://www.johnburtonfoundation.org/

Court Appointed Special Advocates (CASA)

http://www.casaforchildren.org/site/c.mtJSJ7MPIsE/b.5301295/k.BE9A

/Home.htm

WRAP-around services   http://nwi.pdx.edu/wraparound-basics/

ABOUT THE AUTHOR

Regan Matthews is a social worker for a nonprofit foster care and adoption agency. She has previous experience working in fast food chains, retail stores, and other less memorable employment before beginning to work in the field of human services. Ms. Matthews' first experience, after receiving her Bachelors degree from a CSU in the Central Valley, was as a support counselor for a nonprofit foster care and adoption agency where she was employed for about four years. Ms. Matthews also worked with developmentally disabled adults one on one in in-home services for a year. She has been employed with her current agency for nine years. Ms. Matthews has been happily married for 13 years, and has a 21 year old (step) son and five (almost six) year old daughter. Ms. Matthews completed the required 3000 hours of clinical work to sit for the MFT licensure test. However, Ms. Matthews is currently uncertain if she will continue with this path due to other personal dreams and goals of writing.

www.ingramcontent.com/pod-product-compliance
Lightning Source LLC
Chambersburg PA
CBHW070703290526
45790CB00001B/421